Do___
Till H_'s Dead!

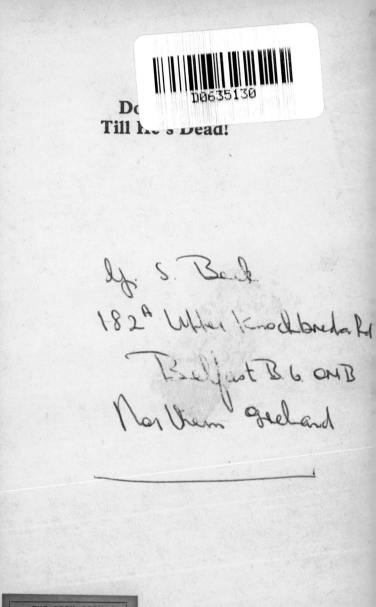

Lj. S. Beck
182ᴬ Upper Knockbreda Rd
Belfast B.6 0NB
Northern Ireland

Have heard Mr Bingham
several times at Centre
Newcastle. Knew his brother
Desmond better.

September 1984

Don't Wait Till He's Dead!

Everybody needs encouragement

NOW!

Derick Bingham

Pickering Paperbacks

First published 1984
by Pickering & Inglis,
3 Beggarwood Lane,
Basingstoke, Hants RG23 7LP,
United Kingdom

ISBN: 0 7208 0575 9

Made and printed in Great Britain by
Hunt Barnard Printing Ltd., Aylesbury, Bucks.

Contents

Acknowledgements

My sincere thanks to my friend Mr Ross Evans and his staff Dorothy Bacon, Norma Burrell, Regina Clarkin, Eleanor Floyd, Margaret Horner, Rosemary Morrow and June Thompson who prepared the manuscript of this book for publication.

To Margaret

Preface

He was sitting there crying like a child. 'You don't know the trouble I'm in,' he said.

My friend was moved to see him weep. 'I'll take you out for a meal next week,' he promised. The next week his distressed friend was dead. He had committed suicide.

Whether it be distressed people or happy ones, failures or successes, and we want to encourage them, for any sakes, *let's do it now*. That is the message of this book.

If with pleasure you are viewing,
Any work a man is doing,
If you like him or you love him, tell him now,
Don't withold your approbation,
Till the parson makes oration,
And he lies with snow white lilies on his brow,
For no matter how you shout it,
He won't really care about it,
He won't know how many teardrops you have shed,
If you think some praise is due him,
Now's the time to slip it to him,
For he cannot read his tomb stone when he's dead.
More than fame and more than money,
Is the comment kind and sunny,
And the hearty warm approval of a friend,
For it gives to life a savour,

And it makes you stronger, braver,
And it gives you heart and spirit to the end,
If he earns your praise – bestow it,
If you like him, let him know it,
Let the words of true encouragement be said,
Do not wait till life is over,
And he's underneath the clover,
For he cannot read his tomb stone when he's dead.

Everybody needs encouragement. We agree to that. Yet, away in the back of our minds we are suspicious of the art of encouragement as if it were admitting to a vain streak in the human condition.

It is no such thing. Encouragement is oxygen to the soul, it is like ice cream in the Sahara, it is like sunshine after rain. For want of it millions upon millions of lives are spent in weary drudgery, going around in ever flagging circles. The child does his sums better next time after his teacher ventures a 'Now-that's-a-good-try-Jimmy'. A teenage girl is visibly lifted in spirit when one day, out of the blue her father says, 'I'm proud of you.' Watch that wife put an extra inch to her step when her husband suddenly springs an 'all-because-the-lady-loves-Milk-Tray' act of kindness upon her! A senior citizen finds that the day is not so long after a junior citizen has taken time to stop by for a 'How's about you'.

An American called Mr Wright gave his two boys Wilbur and Orville a toy flying machine to play with. The world got Concorde. Thomas Edison, friendless and in debt, walked into a building belonging to a telegraph company just as the telegraph stopped working. He was the only person who could put it right and the people there encouraged him to stay. The world recorded sound and got the electric light bulb.

A young man went down one day into a wood and encouraged a depressed outlaw. The young man was called Jonathan, the outlaw, David. The world got, under God, the twenty-third Psalm.

The ministry of encouragement is open to a Christian as it is to no other. He has a new life in Christ, an all powerful Holy Spirit to lead him into all truth, a Heavenly Father who will protect and bless him eternally. If anyone anywhere is qualified and equipped to a ministry of positive and healthy encouragement in a desperately discouraging world, it is the Christian. He is, Christ said, the 'salt of the earth'. He makes life tasty! In his witness he is, above all else, an encourager.

Let no Christian ever say that there is in life no particular ministry for him to fulfil. What everybody needs is encouragement toward what are the best mountains in life to climb, the highest and noblest ambitions to have, the most rewarding treasures to possess. It is a need which every Christian who truly draws from Christ's strength and teaching can supply. Go to it, Christian! The results will utterly amaze you.

Derick Bingham

1: A Community of Encouragement

There is the story told of a man who stood outside a local church building inviting people to come into the services. 'Sorry Sir,' said a passer-by looking at the morose face of the man issuing the invitation, 'I am really sorry but I cannot come in. You see, I have troubles enough of my own!'

The church on earth should be a community of encouragement. Why? Because the church is the body of Christ and each individual member has been converted, God says, to be conformed to the image of his son.[1] If the church members are to be like the Lord Jesus, what was he like? He was ever and always an encourager. So the church should be a community of encouragement.

Study our Lord's attitude to children, to people in trouble, to folks ridden with guilt, to the poor, the sick, the blind. *'Other sheep I have which are not of this fold'*, he told his disciples, *'Them also I must bring.'*[2] The prodigal son must be encouraged back and his good elder brother must join in the encouraging and not stand and sulk if his brother comes home.

Up until his very last moment on earth the Lord was encouraging those around him. *'I am with you always'*, he said as he commissioned his disciples to go into all the world and preach the Gospel.[3] It was adrenalin to their souls.

When we move into the New Testament church what kind of community was it? The people outside of it noticed one great feature of the ne phenomenon. They took note that those Christians *'had been with Jesus'*.[4] We cannot know and be with our Lord Jesus and not encourage others as a result. We encourage others because he encourages us. It was the new-found joy and forgiveness of sins in Christ that drove those first believers all over the face of the earth witnessing to their risen Lord. The people on the outside took note. Thousands upon thousands of them were converted.

Soon, of course, Satan got busy. It would not do to allow such a community of encouragement to go unchallenged. Satan loved to spread confusion and his target was the church. Confusion arose particularly in the matter of public worship which got out of hand. The apostle Paul warned that those on the outside were being discouraged from seeking the Lord by those on the inside. *'Will they not say that you are all mad?'*[5] he warned. There must have been three cheers in Satan's ranks.

Unfortunately such a warning is still needed today. The church across the world instead of being a community of power and the exciting presence of God, has in many places become a very discouraging place to visit in its visible public services. Christians are forgetting their great role to share and pass on the encouragement and blessing God has poured into their lives.

Three Shades of Encouragement

In the New Testament there are three Greek words used for our English word 'encourage'. There is the word *protrepo* which means 'to persuade', to 'urge forward'.[6] The christian church should always be a community which does not allow stagnation. May the church of the living God never become a 'fen of stagnant waters', as the poet William Wordsworth would have put it. God forbid.

The second word used is the word *paramutheomai* meaning 'to stimulate to the discharge of the ordinary duties of life'.[7] This shows clearly that the church should never be afraid of the nitty gritty of life, of 'feet washing' as Jesus taught it. The Saviour moved from divine doctrine to dirty feet in a very short space of time. We would do well to remember this. We must stimulate those who know the Lord to the truth that heavenly minded people should be of great earthly use.

The story is told of the chap who was always going to the local church services. Monday night he was at this service, Tuesday night at that service etc. One evening his exasperated wife challenged him as to where he was going. 'Oh!' he replied, 'Tonight is missionary night. There's a missionary showing a set of slides entitled "Going through Africa with a camel." I'm looking forward to it.'

'You're not going,' his wife said, emphatically.

'And why not?' questioned her husband.

'Because you are going into the kitchen to go through china with a dishcloth!' she replied. It was the nitty gritty for him, indeed.

The third word is the word *paraklesis* which means 'a calling to one's aid', 'to call to one's side'.[8] The sure hope and encouragement of the church is the Christ who comes alongside and aids its needs. So, in turn, the church comes alongside those who need aid and who need the soul-saving Gospel the church is entrusted with proclaiming.

Persuaders, practical people, comforters, the come-alongsiders; they were the community of encouragement that turned the world upside down. How do we measure up? Are these the New Testament principles which mark us?

Sadly so many local churches are more famous for what they stand against rather than what they stand for.

Loving People Needs Talent

One of my favourite writers is the poet Laurie Lee who writes prose like no one I ever came across. In an essay entitled *The Firstborn*[9] he describes his feelings at the birth of his daughter, and few fathers could fail to be moved by the power of his description. I do not agree with everything Lee writes in his essay, but I wholeheartedly acquiesce when he wishes that his newborn daughter would always prefer '*Societies for the Propagation and Promotion*' rather than those '*for the Abolition or Prevention of*'. He also adds that he hopes '*she would avoid like the plague all acts of mob-righteousness, to take cover whenever flags start flying; and to accept her frustrations and faults as her own personal burden, and not to blame them too often, if she can possibly help it, on young or old, whites or coloureds, East, West, Jews, Gentiles, Television, Bingo, Trade Unions, the City, school-milk or British Railways*'. Such words would be well placed on many a church building notice-board!

Lee does add the rider that he hopes his daughter will '*avoid painting by numbers, processed food, processed language, have an antenna for the responses of others and learn that though animals are often much easier to love than men (and both worth it), loving man needs more talent*'.

I find a lot of these qualities in the great New Testament character Lydia. She was the epitome of a persuader, comforter, and a come-along-sider, all rolled in one. Lydia, a dealer in purple cloth, was at a prayer meeting one day by a river. Paul was walking by and noticing the women went over to them and spoke to them of the Lord Jesus. As Lydia listened, '*the Lord opened her heart*'. Did she stop there? Did she simply say 'I'm saved so I shall retire to my home and quietly wait until the Lord comes'?

The first act of Lydia's christian life was an act of encouragement. She persuaded Paul and his friend Silas to make her home their base from which to reach Philippi. Was it a significant act? It is worth seriously noting the vast repercussions of that first encouraging act of Lydia's. The Lord opened her heart and Lydia opened her home and then the Lord opened Philippi to his word and thus the continent of Europe. Lydia was God's highway to a whole continent!!

How can we become such a person? How can we become a community of encouragement? Is it possible? I believe it is. My prayer would be that somewhere in the world some hearts may be touched by the Lord through this little book and as a result be encouraged to encourage. May God show those hearts that they can become his highway to a world of need.

Notes

1. Romans 8.21
2. John 10.16
3. Matthew 28.20
4. Acts 4.13
5. 1 Corinthians 14.23
6. Acts 18.27
7. 1 Thessalonians 5.14
8. Hebrews 6.18
9. Laurie Lee, *I Can't Stay Long* (Penguin Books, 1977, p. 76–85), quoted by permission of Andre Deutsch.

2: It Takes Big Heartedness

I just happen to love the autumn. Fewer people die in 'the fall' than at any other time of year. Often as I stroll in the woods in October, kicking the leaves with my feet and breathing the new nip in the air, words come slowly into my mind; 'Season of mists and mellow fruitfulness', they say. They are the words of a very remarkable young man. His name was John Keats.

Arguably, Keats was the greatest of all English poets. He died when he was twenty five. He left for us poems which haunt and touch the spirit as few other poets have done. Did he get much encouragement to do so in his lifetime? Try a Blackwood's Magazine review of his work:

> 'Mr Keats . . . is only a boy of petty abilities which he has done everything in his power to spoil . . . we venture to make one small prophecy, that his book seller will not a second time venture fifty pounds sterling upon anything he can write. It is a better and a wiser thing to be a starved chemist than a starved poet: so back to the shop, Mr John, back to plasters, pills and ointment boxes'.[1]

He died three years later. Were Blackwood's sorry? They said:

'A Mr John Keats . . . has lately died of consumption, after having written two or three little books of verses, much neglected by the public. His vanity was probably wrung not less than his purse.'

Twenty-seven years later an account of Keats' life and works was published. Thomas Carlyle reviewed it. He wrote four words. He called the work *'Fricassee of dead dog'*.[2]

Why are people so heartless? Why are they so reticent to encourage one another? This is particularly true of people in the same profession. Writers pour scorn on writers, architects pull down other architects, lawyers sneer at lawyers, and even men and women in the gentle art of painting would amaze you by what they say about each other. I once heard an artist advising all who would paint to do so from the heart and not the head. He urged artists to get into the environment of what they would paint; if they would paint miners then they must go down mines. This all sounded good advice until I heard him say something which utterly amazed me: *'If you want to be a good artist,'* he concluded, *'stay away from other artists!'*

John Ruskin called Constable's painting *'the mere blundering of a clever peasant'*.[3] Turner, suggested one critic got his tremendous effects *'as if by throwing handfuls of white, blue and red at canvas and letting what would stick, stick!'*.[4]

It is no different in any profession. Tchaikovsky called Brahms *'giftless'*.[5] *'Wagner's music is better than it sounds'*, said Nye.[6] On and on, works of beauty, originality and inspiration are torn apart by those who would paint it, write it, sculpt it, speak it, preach it, if only they could.

Preach it? No group of men tear each other verbally apart as heartlessly as preachers. Encouragement from preacher to preacher is often as rare as sleep on a 747. I know, because I happen to be one and the son of one. The very people who are meant to be out there encouraging people towards 'things above' often seem to leave encouraging words to each other 'down below'. If they feel such words rising they seem to somehow stick in their throats. That they agree theologically makes no difference. In fact the more they seem to agree theologically the less seems to be the personal encouragement.

My mother once gave me a word of advice. 'In the presence of a preacher don't praise another one too much, it makes your listener jealous.' She knew what went on. She was being honest.

Christians Who Persecute Christians!

In every century it seems to be the same. Hudson Taylor, the intrepid young Christian who took the Gospel to China, was bitterly discouraged by the tongues of fellow Christians who were ostensibly doing the same work. Their pitiless and heartless criticisms of the stripling who was destined far-to-surpass his critics in fame and usefulness is mind-boggling to read.

Amy Carmichael was a gentle Irish christian poetess and author who did a significant work for God in India. If you have never read her books I urge you to get your hands on them and you will not regret it. Amy protected children in India from the wicked practice of parents who sold their children to heathen priests for evil purposes. Hundreds of children lived to thank God for her protection, but the christian missionary establishment pitilessly criticised Amy for daring to enter a world to which the ruling British administration was turning a blind eye. Amy 'rocked the boat' and fellow-Christians had it in for her!

I think of the present-day christian author Elisabeth Elliot whose husband Jim was murdered by the Auca Indians in Ecuador in 1956 as he tried to reach them with the Gospel. Recently Elisabeth was asked to write a biography about a great christian leader and she tried to be honest in her writing and face the fact that he had his faults as well as his great qualities. Such writing is right in line with biblical biography. Was Elisabeth praised for trying to be scriptural? She has written that she was, in fact, strongly criticised by Christians for her honest efforts!

I have often taken great comfort in the fact that all men and women of God have drawn fire from christian discouragers. Again and again godly people all over the world tell me that the most heart-breaking discouragement they ever receive is from fellow-Christians! Incredible as it is, the fact is startlingly true.

Who in the last century bore a more faithful and joyous witness for the Lord Jesus than Charles Haddon Spurgeon? Millions have found Christ down the years through his spoken and written witness. What encouragement did he receive? Try this, said to have been written by a man called James Wells in a publication called *The Earthen Vessel*, who signed his article, '*Job*'. '*I have, most solemnly have, my doubts as to the divine reality of his* (Spurgeon's) *conversion.*'[7] The rest of his article would amaze you as he tried to prove his point! Is it any wonder then that Spurgeon's young wife hung a text above his bed which read '*Blessed are you when they revile and persecute you and say all kinds of evil against you falsely for my sake.*'[8]

The twentieth century has not changed men's hearts; the genuine Holy-Spirit-led encourager is a rare occurrence, even among those who preach God's word. The discouragers are as numerous as the flies of summer.

My friend Ian Barclay often speaks of a particularly gifted

man about whom he wrote a recent *Christian Herald* article:

'*Let me tell you about the young man who, I feel, could have been one of the great evangelists of the world. He was a regular preacher to the poor in and around London about a hundred years ago. There are many references to his preaching in his letters. In one dated October 13, 1876, he wrote,* "Last Monday I was again at Richmond and my subject was *'He has sent me to preach the Gospel to the poor,'* but whoever wants to preach the Gospel must first carry it in his own heart." *His favourite hymn was* "Tell me the old, old story of Jesus and his love"; *and his favourite reading, apart from the Bible, was the works of Charles H. Spurgeon, and in particular a book called* Little Jewels.

The young man was born in Zundert in Holland in 1853. His father was a Lutheran pastor, and after he left school in 1869 he started work for a firm of art dealers in The Hague. In 1873 he had the chance to travel and moved to London and the Southampton Street branch of his firm. He was a typical young businessman of the time. You could see him any day in a formal suit and top hat, walking from his lodgings in Kensington to The Strand.

He fell in love with Ursula Loyer, his landlady's daughter, but she was already engaged and laughed at his obvious affection for her. He turned to Jesus for consolation, and found in him such spiritual blessing that he was soon helping the local Methodist minister by taking meetings in Turnham Green and Petersham. The conviction grew that he should be a full-time evangelist, so in 1877 he returned to his native Holland to commence training for the ministry.

He found the academic demands of the theological college in Amsterdam too demanding and moved to a newly opened school for evangelists in Brussels. He soon found great

*success in preaching to the poor by dressing like a peasant
and living in their company. He was concerned for their
needs; he washed their clothes, he cared for their sick and
consoled their dying, and led them to Christ.*

*His dress and methods were superbly Christ-like and
undoubtedly incarnational in that he went down-and-out to
win the lost. But the church leaders of the day would have
nothing to do with him, and forced him to leave the ministry;
eventually he was even to lose his faith. He went back into
the world of art dealing and tried his hand at a little
painting. His name was Vincent van Gogh. If he could paint
as he did – think how he might have preached? If he could
depict a sunflower with such power on a canvas, just think
how well he would have proclaimed the Son of God from a
pulpit!*

*For me one of the saddest aspects of his life as an artist
centres on a painting called "The Bible". It shows a Bible
lying open at Isaiah 53. Nearby is a candle that has gone
out. In front of the unused Bible is a novel by Emile Zola
called "La Joie de Vivre" that is clearly well read. How
regrettable it is when the light goes from the message of God's
Suffering Servant, and a novel shows us the way to a zest of
life.*

Vincent van Gogh said, "I must tell you that with
evangelists it is the same as with artists. There is an old
academic school, tyrannical men, who wear prejudice and
conventions." *May God give us grace to support and
encourage openly all evangelists who preach the Gospel of the
Lord Jesus Christ.'*

It takes what I am calling 'big heartedness' for a person to
overcome jealousy, envy, division and personality
differences to reach out and become an encourager. The

Bible gives a great illustration of this rare ministry. His name was Jonathan.

Jonathan was the son of Saul, King of Israel. Unfortunately King Saul had got away from God into disobedience and had become a rather pathetic figure. A man out of the will of God is not a power for God, no matter what his social standing. Satan was having great victory among God's people and he was having it through a giant of a man called Goliath.

The way David tackled Goliath is history. What is often forgotten is *the reaction of Jonathan* to the great events in the valley of Elah. Saul's reaction is legendary, he was so jealous of David he tried more than thirty times to kill him. But what of Jonathan? If he had any jealousy he put out that hell spark in a sea of faith because we read; *'Jonathan took off the robe that was on him and gave it to David with his armour, even to his sword and his bow and his belt'.*[9]

Here was encouragement of the highest order. As Jonathan saw all the events of that greatest of days in David's life he was just so downright big-hearted about it all. He took all the insignia of his high position and gave them, immediately, to David. He did not go around moaning that this new star in their midst was a threat to his position, which he certainly was. Jonathan did not play the old we-will-wait-and-see game. Mr Great Heart, John Bunyan would have called him. Genuine, godly love never ever looks on another believer's success as a threat, it looks on it as a blessing. It gets right in there giving all the possible support it can possibly give, immediately.

Is this the kind of love Christians show to other Christians when God's blessing suddenly descends upon their gifts and talents? Often Satan sees to it that we act like Saul in our hearts instead of Jonathan. Let's be honest. I have often heard, and so have you, pitiless criticism of individuals, upon whom the hand of God is so obviously resting, by others and the reason is (far be it from them to admit) pitiless jealousy.

Was Jonathan's big heartedness a mere passing act originating in the emotion of David's great moment of faith and disappearing later when David proved that he too could get out of God's will? It was no mere passing act. Right through Saul's fierce opposition to David, Jonathan remained David's great source of comfort and encouragement. In 1 Samuel chapter 20 we read the moving covenant these two men made regarding how David promised he would even care for Jonathan's children should Jonathan die. This was a deep act of commitment in friendship and encouragement, and it has its modern counterparts. Sitting recently at the Filey Convention, I was chatting to Dave and Sue Foster who live in Switzerland and who do such wonderful work for their Lord all over Europe. They told me that when first they stepped out, by faith, to serve God in extensive christian work, a couple they knew covenanted to pray for them, to help them and to look after their children for life should anything happen to their parents. I have a friend who from the very moment I gave up school teaching to go preaching and teaching God's word has never failed to stand by me through 'thick and thin' over all these years of christian work, and I mean stand by me, even when I am wrong, which is all too often.

Accepting Encouragement Graciously Isn't Easy

When people reach out to strengthen and encourage us it is not always easy to accept such encouragement graciously. We can be embarrassed, our pride can be demolished, our 'but-I-can-cope' attitude can be challenged. Most Christians are usually on the giving end, not the receiving. Charles Swindoll illustrates this point with a memorable story from his life and ministry:

'A man in our church congregation drove over to our home with his Christmas gift to our family. Not something wrapped up in bright paper with a big ribbon but a thoughtful gift of love demonstrated by washing all the windows of our home. I was studying that Saturday morning at my office at the church building as my wife and children welcomed him in. He quietly began doing the job. I drove up later that morning and immediately noticed his car out front. I wondered if there was perhaps some need (there I was again, thinking like I usually do).

The kids met me at the door with the news that Phil (not his real name) was washing our windows. My immediate response, of course, was surprise. I knew he was a busy husband and father with many more things to do than clean my windows. I went to the patio and saw his smiling face.

"Phil, what's going on? Man, I can't believe this!" Still smiling, his response, "Chuck, I just wanted to do this for you and your family, Merry Christmas!"

"Hey, Phil" (I'm now a little embarrassed), "what do you say you finish up the patio doors and we'll get the rest, okay?"

"Nope. I'd like to go all the way around."

"Gee, thanks man . . . but you've got lots of other things more important to do. Tell you what, you get all the downstairs, and the kids and I will get the upstairs."

"No, I'd really like to get up there too."

"Well, uh – why don't you get the outside all the way around and we'll get the inside?"

Phil paused, looked directly at me and said, "Chuck! I want to wash ALL the windows, upstairs and downstairs, *inside and outside—every one of them. You are always giving. For a change, I'd like you to receive." Suddenly, I realised what a battle I have graciously receiving others' gifts.'*[10]

When Heroes Are Unheroic

Giving encouragement to someone after we see him do some good thing is great, but what happens when he lets us down and acts stupidly and is an embarrassment? Jonathan, again, is a wonderful example of a man who was big-hearted to encourage when everything went dead-wrong.

The story of David's panic is told simply (and warts-and allishly!) in 1 Samuel chapter 21. David flees to Nob where about eighty of Israel's priests are living. He takes his eyes off the Lord, and when the godly Ahimelech asks him why he is alone, he lies to him. He says he has come on the King's business. Then, amazingly, David asks Ahimelech: *'Is there not here on hand a spear or a sword? For I have brought neither my sword nor my weapons with me, because the King's business required haste.'*

It was another lie, but it was also an incredible request. In modern terms it is tantamount to going to your local pastor's house and asking, 'Excuse me, or, sorry to bother, but would you have any guns?'

There is a very dramatic and emotional turn in the events of that sad day in David's life. Ahimelech turns to him and says that he does actually have a sword on the premises. *'The sword of Goliath the Philistine, whom you killed in the valley of Elah, there it is, wrapped in a cloth behind the ephod. If you take it, take it. For there is no other except that one here.'*

What is he saying? He is saying that David did not slay Goliath with a sword, he killed him with a sling and a stone guided by faith. After the stone had done its deadly work, David had taken Goliath's sword and cut Goliath's head off. That sword had been taken by the priests and kept at Nob as a national treasure. People would look at it and no doubt comment on its significance. It was a symbol of what faith in God could do. Now David wanted that sword to defend himself against Saul. What a reversal of faith in a man! They are sad words, some of the saddest in the Old Testament. And David said, *'There is none like it: give it to me.'*

Soon David has fled to Goliath's city and is living under the security of God's enemies. The people begin talking about him: *'Is not this David?'* they ask. David, hopelessly compromised in his testimony for God pretended he was mad, scrabbled on the doors of the city gates, *'let his saliva fall down on his beard'* and was promptly thrown out of the city.

If we had seen David that day we would not have believed him to be the same man. We would have given him up. It takes big-heartedness to spiritually encourage a very successful believer but it takes even greater courage to encourage a successful believer who has, suddenly, made an absolute mess of his life. Watch Jonathan in action. In 1 Samuel 23.16–18 we read that *'Jonathan, Saul's son, arose and went to David into the wood and strengthened his hand in God. And he said to him,* "Do not fear for the hand of Saul my father shall not find you. You shall be King over Israel and I shall be next to you. Even my father Saul knows that." *So the two of them made a covenant before the Lord. And David stayed in the woods and Jonathan went to his own house.'*

Jonathan's encouragement of David was unconditional, neither David's great gifts nor appalling weaknesses held back this man of God from what he felt to be his duty. He encouraged him to depend on God. David, who had encouraged a nation to depend on God now needed someone to encourage him to depend on God! And this is the point.

Can I ever forget listening to the great Martyn Lloyd Jones once preach at Cambridge University? I can hear him yet in my mind expounding 1 Corinthians 14 to that packed audience of students in the Union. They were late arriving: *'I wonder, were you late for the hockey match this afternoon?'* he said quietly . . . He was not afraid of his audience! And what of the conversations we had in private that week-end? I was never the same again. Tens of thousands around the world thank God for the Doctor's gift. Yet strangely, a preaching friend told me he once thanked the Doctor for his ministry and mentioned how much he had enjoyed it. *'Thank you'*, said the one time assistant to the King's physician, *'Thank you for your word of encouragement. Very few people say such things to me.'* May our generation be different. Let's be big-hearted Jonathans wherever we go.

Notes

1. Believed to have been written by John Lockhart and John Wilson, *Blackwoods Magazine*, August 1818.
2. Thomas Carlyle (1795–1881), Review of Monkton Milnes' *Life of Keats*.
3. John Ruskin (1891–1900), *Lectures on Landscape*, 'Colour'.
4. *Literary Gazette*, May 1842.
5. Tchaikovsky, *Diary 9*, October 1886.
6. Bill Nye (1850–1896), American writer.
7. *The Earthen Vessel*, December 1854.
8. Matthew 5.11–12
9. 1 Samuel 18.4
10. C. R. Swindoll, *Improving Your Serve* (Hodder and Stoughton, 1983), quoted by permission of Hodder and Stoughton, p. 169.

3: Mr Encouragement

He came from Cyprus and his name means 'The son of encouragement'.[1] His father called him Joses, I call him 'Mr Encouragement', the Apostles called him Barnabas.

While shopping in Dublin one Christmas and watching the Santa Claustrophobia around me I noticed out of the corner of my eye a very famous gentleman shopping. His name is Eamonn Andrews and he had a chat. Eamonn is famous across the United Kingdom for his television programme where he suddenly comes up to an unsuspecting person and says 'This is your life'. Then follows a fascinating array of people and recalled situations from the subject's life, revealing memorabilia of all kinds. Can I be Eamonn for a moment and say to this great Bible character Barnabas, 'This is your life'? Bible characters are not there as mere historical footnotes. They are there for our learning and if anyone can teach us about encouragement, Barnabas can. What qualities did he have?

He was generous. The very first time we meet him in Scripture we read that Barnabas *'having land, sold it and brought the money and laid it at the Apostles' feet'*.[2] In ancient times Cyprus was famous for its mines, its wheat, its oil, its figs and honey. Barnabas the Cypriot certainly possessed possessions but the happy thing was that his possessions did not possess him.

Nowhere in Scripture are Christians forbidden the

ownership of possessions but the point is that Barnabas was not tight-fisted.

Mean People Have a Look About Them

No tight-fisted, mean Christian ever had a great ministry of encouragement. They are no good at it. Miserly, ungenerous spirits do not warm our hearts when we are bereaved, or heart-broken, or depressed or worried. Mean people have a look about them. They are cold in spirit and very, very, critical. There is a happy, joyful abandon to a life of giving in Mr Encouragement. He gives you of his time, food of his table; somehow you know he is glad to see you. 'No trouble at all' is his watch word and, if he has a wife, you will find she can make you a cup of coffee almost as quick as you can say 'Barnabas'! *'We make a living by what we get,'* wrote Winston Churchill, *'but we make a life by what we give.'*[3] What a life Barnabas made!

Barnabas was also a man of great courage. We need courage to encourage. How often I have found in the Lord's work that when encouragement is needed by someone it takes that extra inch of courage to reach out your hand, to lift that pen, to lift that telephone and open your heart. Sometimes it takes great courage.

If Idi Amin[4] came to faith in Christ as Saviour would we rush over to encourage him? I doubt it. Here was a Pharisee named Saul, a brilliant Jewish academic agreeing to men battering the gentle Stephen to death. Saul was at that time making *'havoc of the church, entering into every house and having men and women committed to prison'*. Suddenly and dramatically Saul is converted to Christ and is telling everyone that the Lord Jesus is the only way!

After preaching Christ at Damascus and some time had elapsed Saul goes up to Jerusalem to join the Christians, '*but*', says God's word, '*they were all afraid of him and did not believe that he was a disciple*'.[5] A few dissenters would not have been a big hindrance but when Peter and John and Andrew, Philip, Thomas, Bartholomew, James, Simon and Judas, James' brother, and Mary and the Lord's own believing brothers[6] and all the rest of the believers in Jerusalem say, '*We don't believe the man is a believer at all*' – the chances of fellowship are pretty thin!

In my land we have this great problem; men who condone violence and men who have been deeply involved in violence sometimes become Christians. Few there are who take them to their hearts. It is no easy business, if you ask me it is a very uneasy business. But Mr Encouragement has courage. He is in there quickly ready to defend a young believer with a history that is not good.

With courage Barnabas faces criticism and prejudice (the most subtle enemy of truth) and, records Luke, '*But Barnabas took him and brought him to the Apostles. And he declared to them how he had seen the Lord on the road and that he had spoken to him and how he had . . . and he was . . . and he spoke . . .*' The words of Barnabas seem to trip over one another as with great enthusiasm he defends Saul of Tarsus! The Christians believed him too. It is interesting to muse upon the question that if there had been no Barnabas, would we have had the majestic epistle to the Romans, the joyous letter to the Philippians, the mystical letter to the Ephesians, the fetter-breaking epistle to the Galatians and the eternally practical two letters to the Corinthians? Would Timothy ever have read Paul's words of advice to him? God always has his Barnabases around at the right moment. Barnabas could never have written Paul's letters, but he could minister to Paul when no one else wanted to know him and then, my, how the letters came! *We never know where a word of encouragement goes*. Barnabas never reckoned that a man sitting on that Jumbo Jet at thirty-nine thousand feet over the Atlantic today would pull out a copy of Paul's letters and read them. Barnabas never knew that millions upon millions upon millions of copies of these letters would, in the twentieth century, be found in hotel rooms, doctors' surgeries, army barracks, prison cells, presidents' desks, housewives' corners and children's schoolbags! Mr Encouragement has a ministry which circles the globe. Encouragers are great strategists. When they set their sights on a man to encourage him – look out!

The Unsectarian Barnabas

Barnabas had another quality which all who seek a ministry of encouragement should cultivate. God knows it is a quality which is hard to have. Barnabas had an unsectarian spirit.

Sectarianism is a curse. By 'party spirit' Satan has blasted the unity of born-again people to smithereens. I have never met a Christian anywhere who had a sectarian spirit and was, at the same time, given to a ministry of true, godly, enthusiastic, christian encouragement. Barnabas was greatly used by God to sway thousands away from the wretched thing.

Not that he did not have traces of sectarianism in him. The Bible is very careful to show us that its heroes are men and women just like us. Let's trace the story carefully. We shall learn much on the way.

After Stephen had been martyred, a great persecution arose against believers and they scattered far and wide, witnessing for the Lord wherever they went. Some of Barnabas' christian fellow countrymen from Cyprus found themselves at Antioch in Syria, but they would only preach the word to Jews. One day they happened to meet some

Greeks and, sinking their prejudices they broke out and preached about the Lord Jesus to them. Immediately many of them were converted! When news of it reached the church at Jerusalem they dispatched Barnabas to see what was going on. He, encourager as he was, immediately rejoiced with his generous, courageous, unsectarian spirit.

> 'When he came and had seen the grace of God, he was glad, and encouraged them all that with purpose of heart they should continue with the Lord. For he was a good man, full of the Holy Spirit and of faith. And a great many people were added to the Lord.'[7]

'He . . . encouraged them all': this was the ministry of Barnabas at Antioch. Could you and I not make it ours wherever we go in these difficult days? 'For', adds Luke, 'he was a good man full of the Holy Spirit and of faith.'

'Then Barnabas departed for Tarsus to seek Saul; and when he had found him, he brought him to Antioch.' Notice that Barnabas was, like the Old Testament Jonathan before him, an encourager of others and knew no jealousy in his heart. If he did he successfully overcame it. As Alexander Whyte once wrote,

> 'Barnabas had not been long in Antioch till he became convinced that Antioch was very soon to hold the key of the whole christian position . . . in all Barnabas' knowledge of men, and, it was not narrow, he knew only one man who was equal to the great emergency at Antioch, and that man was no other than Saul of Tarsus. But, then, Saul was comparatively young as yet; he was not much known and he was not much trusted. And shall Barnabas take on himself the immense responsibility and, indeed, risk of sending for Saul of Tarsus and bringing him to Antioch? . . . There are

supreme moments in the field when an officer of original genius, and of requisite strength of character will determine to stake all and do some bold deed, on his own single responsibility . . . he will thus win the battle. Antioch must have Saul of Tarsus; and Barnabas, taking counsel with no one but himself, set out to Tarsus to seek for Saul. . . . To have the heart to discover a more talented man than yourself, and then to have the heart to go to Tarsus for him and to make way for him in Antioch, is far better than to have all Saul's talents and all the praise and all the rewards of those talents to yourself . . .: "He must increase, but I must decrease," *said Barnabas to himself . . . as he set his face steadfastly to go down to Tarsus.*[8]

For a whole year Paul and Barnabas met with the church at Antioch and taught many people. But there were problems. The sectarian streak in Barnabas was temptingly encouraged by Satan at Antioch. In the midst of all the blessing Peter arrived.

'But when Peter had come to Antioch, I withstood him to his face, because he was to be blamed; for before certain men came from James, he would eat with the Gentiles; but when they came, he withdrew and separated himself, fearing those who were of the circumcision. And the rest of the Jews also played the hypocrite with him, so that even Barnabas was carried away with their hypocrisy.[9]

Poor Barnabas! That cosy feeling that comes when we are identified with a certain party or school of thought swamped his better judgement. Barnabas was almost overcome by the fear of dissenting brethren around him. But he overcame it. He rose above their narrow squabblings and obeyed his Lord, doing away with the prejudice that would have tied him to preaching only to his fellow Jews. Was he not glad? What was the result? It has great significance for us all because we read *'And the disciples were first called "Christians" at Antioch.'*[10]

That lovely name 'Christian' came, then, as a result of Barnabas' courage. Because of the non-sectarian spirit of Barnabas, people no longer referred to 'Jews' or 'Gentiles' in the ranks of the believers. Now they were all Christians – followers of Christ. Could a ministry of encouragement have a higher reward?

In the same Bible chapter we read that in response to the great famine that came in the days of Claudius Caesar *'The disciples, each according to his ability, determined to send relief to the brethren dwelling in Judea. This they also did, and sent it to the elders by the hands of Barnabas and Saul.'* Encouragers can be trusted!

Helpful Wolf Repellent

Self-image is a real problem for some people, identity as individuals in an uncaring world is difficult. But it should not be the case with Christians. Christians know that their Lord called them 'the salt of the earth' and 'the light of the world'[11]! When Paul and Barnabas faced a hostile, blaspheming crowd of Jews, they, with great boldness, identified themselves as the fulfilment of Isaiah's prophecy which said *'I have set you to be a light to the Gentiles, that you should be for salvation to the ends of the earth.'*[12] They knew their calling and they were not ashamed of it. Neither should we be.

The image that the people at Lystra had of Barnabas and Paul was, unfortunately, the wrong one. Because of the power of their preaching the people thought they were gods. They called Barnabas, *Zeus* and Paul, *Hermes*. They wanted to make sacrifices to them. But the men of God would have none of it. With vigour they ran in among the people, crying, *'Men, why are you doing these things? We also are men with the same nature as you, and preach to you that you should turn from these vain things to the living God.'*[13] Mr Encouragement is always, when in the Spirit, humble.

'I used to think', wrote F. B. Meyer, *'that God's gifts were on shelves one above the other and that the taller we grow in Christian character the more easily we could reach them. I now find that God's gifts are on shelves one beneath the other and that it is not a question of growing taller but of stooping lower.'*

Encouragers never run when they see wolves coming – even wolves in sheep's clothing.[14] When wolves from Judea came ravaging God's flock with the heinous doctrine that unless a certain Jewish rite had been submitted to, no one could be saved, Barnabas didn't run. Barnabas who, like his master, was no hireling, stood up against them for the truth of the Gospel. Later at the Council of Jerusalem, called to consider the matter, Barnabas helped carry the day. Mr Encouragement is always a great wolf-repellent. Let us always have him around in a crisis.

But all Bible examples of men, probably with the exception of Joseph, have a mark against them. The amazing Paul and Barnabas had a sickening row. Satan is a dirty fighter and, because of a dispute over whether or not they should take a young Christian on one of their evangelistic tours, the two mighty christian leaders parted. *'Then the contention became so sharp that they parted from one another'*,[15] says Luke. We never read that they met again. Satan is an angel of light and so blinds even the.

godliest with the good of their position that sometimes they do not see the better.

There is one interesting point, though. Barnabas took the young Christian in question, Mark, with him on parting from Paul. Mark had a history of getting out of the kitchen when it was too hot, he had a history of desertion in the face of pressure. That is why Paul wouldn't have him.

Yet, in Paul's very last and moving letter from Rome, written when he faced execution, he pleads with young Timothy; *'Get Mark and bring him with you: for he is useful to me for ministry.'*[16] I rather think Mr Encouragement was top-rate in the ministry of restoring wayward young Christians and pointing them to higher things. Paul obviously thought so.

Barnabas – preacher, teacher, apostle and encourager. We salute you, Mr Encouragement!

Notes

1. Acts 4.36 RSV
2. Acts 4.36–37
3. Wirt/Beckstorm: *Living Quotations for Christians* (Hodder and Stoughton, 1974), quoted by permission of Hodder and Stoughton, p. 84.
4. Former ruthless dictator of Uganda and persecutor of thousands of believers.
5. Acts 9.26
6. Acts 1.14
7. Acts 11.23
8. Alexander Whyte: *Bible characters* (Marshall, Morgan and Scott, 1972), p. 138.
9. Galatians 2.11
10. Acts 11.26
11. Matthew 5.13–14
12. Acts 13.47
13. Acts 14.15
14. Matthew 7.15
15. Acts 15.36–39
16. 2 Timothy 4.11

4: When Encouragement Hurts

A Christian I knew once got into very serious trouble. No one, and I mean it, would talk to him or counsel him about his problem. Nobody wanted to know.

One day when praying about the matter I felt this sudden urge and conviction that the Lord wanted me to talk to him. It may sound facetious but I can honestly say that my whole spirit rebelled against the idea. Satan pitched in with an accusation: 'But you have often sinned grievously yourself, you hypocrite! What right have you to talk to him?' Thoughts of Calvary and the forgiveness of sins I received there came rushing in to counteract Satan's attack, so, in Calvary love, I knocked on his door.

Gently we talked about the problem, ever so gently. His tears flowed; hot and scalding ones they were. God drew near. Such encouragement back to a steadier path hurts. Seldom is it given without tears being shed and sometimes the encourager sheds as many as the encouraged. When I now see the way God has worked in that man's life, whose door I had knocked in great weakness, I breathe a prayer of thanks for the encouragement that hurts to help.

So far in our consideration of the subject of encouragement we have been thinking of the encouragement that is necessary when someone is doing something well. Now I want to concentrate on the encouragement that is necessary when someone is grievously astray and needs encouragement to repent toward God and to follow on in the pathway of God's will.

Nathan: The Man Whose Encouragement Hurt

The epitome of such a ministry is found in the great but costly action of Nathan who faced King David with the great wrong in his life. We read about it in 2 Samuel 12.1–15:

'*Then the Lord sent Nathan to David. And he came to him, and said to him: "There were two men in one city, one rich and the other poor.*

"The rich man had exceedingly many flocks and herds. But the poor man had nothing, except one little ewe lamb which he had bought and nourished; it grew up together with him and with his children. It ate of his own food and drank from his own cup and lay in his bosom; and it was like a daughter to him.

"And a traveller came to the rich man, who refused to take from his own flock and from his own herd to prepare one for the wayfaring man who had come to him; but he took the poor man's lamb and prepared it for the man who had come to him."

Then David's anger was greatly aroused against the man, and he said to Nathan, "as the Lord lives, the man who has done this shall surely die!

"And he shall restore fourfold for the lamb, because he did this thing and because he had no pity."

Then Nathan said to Daivd, "You are the man! Thus says the Lord God of Israel: I anointed you King over Israel, and I delivered you from the hand of Saul. I gave you your master's house and your master's wives into your keeping, and gave you the house of Israel and Judah. And if that had been too little, I also would have given you much more!

"Why have you despised the commandment of the Lord, to do evil in his sight? You have killed Uriah the Hittite with the sword; you have killed him with the sword of the people of Ammon.

"Now therefore, the sword shall never depart from your house, because you have despised me, and have taken the wife of Uriah the Hittite to be your wife.

"Thus says the Lord: Behold, I will raise up adversity against you from your own house; and I will take your wives before your eyes and give them to your neighbour, and he shall lie with your wives in the sight of this sun. For you did it secretly, but I will do this thing before all Israel, before the sun."

Then David said to Nathan, "I have sinned against the Lord." And Nathan said to David, "The Lord also has put away your sin, you shall not die.

"However, because by this deed you have given great occasion to the enemies of the Lord to blaspheme, the child also who is born to you shall surely die."

Then Nathan departed to his house.'

The first and very necessary qualification Nathan had to encourage David back to repentance and faith was that *he was led by the Lord* to do it: *'Then the Lord sent Nathan to David.'* This qualification truly makes all the difference. We all know too well the 'bunglers' who walk all over a problem with their big feet and who know nothing about sensitivity. But, have we ever experienced the powerful touch of a man or woman sent from God into our lives with the encouragement that hurts to help? God sends them in the rarest circumstances. I know, God has sent them to me.

I want above all things to be practical in this book; to get to the nitty-gritty of life. The best way I feel I can communicate the experience of a person sent from God into one's life is to share a prayer I once wrote down. Paul wrote some prayers down, and so did Job and Nehemiah and Moses and Augustine and A. W. Tozer and John Bunyan, and many others; so, I am in good company! This prayer concerns a man who was sent by God to me one winter's night.

All On A Winter's Evening

'Lord, he was a very down-to-earth man. Spade is a spade man. It was at the end of a winter's evening journey that he began to talk to me about being careful with those on the way up because I might have to pass them on the way down.

There was something about his talking, Lord. Suddenly, as he sat in that car, I was aware that it was not just the man who was talking; you were using him, Lord. I heard your voice through his straight-as-an-arrow talk.

Preachers, Lord, he was talking about preachers. He did not claim to be one himself, no, no: his claim was that he had known quite a few (forgive me, Lord, for going on about preachers but you made me into one).

He spoke of great days of your blessing on their lives, Lord. He saw it himself. Great crowds attended their preaching; many were saved by your grace. People had their faith strengthened. There was much rejoicing.

Then, Lord, he spoke of the way he had seen them slide, Lord. They began in their popularity to forget about their dependence upon you alone. He told me that when they were looking to you for their next pound, they were mighty for you, Lord. Then they began to have plenty of pounds, Lord. Ever so slowly they did not seem to have the same grip, power, influence-for-you, Lord. It was hard to define. People began to notice the difference; even walked out of their services in disgust. The salt had lost its savour, Lord. Those preachers became almost useless.

And it was not always materialistic prosperity, Lord. It would seem that they were great until they discovered that they were great, Lord.

There was a chap driving the car that night (you remember, Lord) and after the man of God had departed and he had driven me home that chap put his head on the driving wheel and cried. Cried like a broken hearted little girl, Lord. Only he was a big, strong man. He was frightened of what could happen to his work for you if he got proud.

Me, Lord, how did I feel? I was wondering all the time if the man in the car were not an angel visiting me, unawares. I got the message, Lord. Thanks.

Thoughts of Paul kept flooding my mind. "Lest when I have preached to others I myself should be a castaway."[1] Paul was obviously admitting that he was frightened of becoming like a fellow on an island in some great ocean, Lord. Alive but useless. A castaway with a saved soul but a wasted life. I thought of David, Lord. Proud? He thought he was so powerful he could do what he liked as he strode on the rooftop that day. He forgot about you, Lord and the sword never departed out of his house until the day they buried him.

I thought of Samson, Lord; he had the strength and the gifts to be a great spiritual blessing to Israel but he squandered it all. He was a 'HE man with a SHE weakness.'[2] Israel was just in the same state the day he died as the day he was born. What a spectacle he was at the end with his eyes gouged out, Lord. Frightening, Lord. Poor Samson.

So, Lord, this confession is that all too often we seem to forget that all the gifts, or talents, or money or prosperity or whatever we have come right from your hand, Lord. The proud men in the christian church at Corinth forgot that, Lord. I seem to remember that another group of Christians

*in the Book of Revelation were the same. Left their first love
for you, Lord. They thought they were rich and had need of
nothing and were, all the time, cold and blind and naked.
You said you would spew them out of your mouth, Lord.
Aye, Lord, the fairest flower in paradise was humility but it
was the very first to fade. Right, Lord?'*

It Is All In The Timing

Nathan was sent by God to David but notice God's timing.
It was at least a year since David's dreadful acts. There had
been no word to David in all of those months but now
Nathan arrives. When we go to encourage someone towards
a better path let us watch our timing. God's timing is not
always ours. There is a time to warn an erring Christian but
there is also a time when it is most inappropriate. As sure as
daylight when you hear a person beginning his warning or
admonition with the words 'This is probably not the time
nor the place but . . .' you can be absolutely sure it isn't!
Nathan's timing was right.

It is, of course, not always *what* you say, but *the way you
say it*. When our Lord was wanting to give to the woman at
the well the encouragement that would hurt to help he did
not begin with the statement *'go call your husband',*[3]
knowing very well that she had had five husbands and that
her present companion was not her husband. He talked to
her about water! From language the woman understood, he
gently let her to repentance and faith.

Nathan chose his words carefully and was very wise in the
way he approached David. There are few men in the world
who could approach the chief executive of a country and
accurately accuse him of adultery without ever using the
word. Nathan did. Nathan knew his man. The shepherd's
crook and the king's sceptre were both appropriate to David

and Nathan winged his words home to the man along shepherding emotions. The man who wrote the twenty third psalm perfectly understood Nathan's parable and reacted just as Nathan knew he would: *'As the Lord lives, the man who has done this shall surely die.'*

'You are the man,' said Nathan with holy boldness. Notice the economy of words, the incisive, careful, sure-of-his-facts way Nathan brought the Lord's message to David.

David's reaction to Nathan's ministry is most touching. Heartbroken, the King sees that he has sinned before the Lord and repents with tears. The psalms he wrote of this experience are legendary. Yet Nathan nowhere apologises for the heavy message of God's judgement he brought. How often when we have to deliver a message of warning from God we are tripping over ourselves in order to take away its cutting edge. We are all so afraid of telling it like it is.

There was forgiveness, too: *'The Lord also has put away your sin; you shall not die,'* said Nathan. The encourager, no matter how dark the day, always brings a message of hope. Those who encourage and who come speaking of God's forgiveness are in effect only beggars telling other beggars where to find bread. They know, as Betsie Ten Boom said in the Ravensbruck concentration camp in World War II that there is *'no pit so deep that Christ is not deeper still'*. Restoration for a backslider must always be kept in mind no matter how complex the problem of his failure. We must ponder well the words of Paul: *'Brethren, if a man is overtaken in any trespass, you who are spiritual restore such a person in a spirit of gentleness, considering yourself lest you also be tempted.'*[4]

On Holding A Person's Respect

The success of Nathan's ministry can be clearly seen

months later. The night Nathan went home after delivering God's message was not, I believe, a night of gloating or I-told-you-so talk. In the months that followed Nathan still held David's friendship and respect and obviously showed his love for him. This is proved when David and Bathsheba had a little boy called Solomon, because Nathan gave Solomon a special name. He called him *Jedidiah*, which means 'beloved of the Lord'.

Surely the one great mark of truly successful spiritual shepherding of wayward sheep is how the sheep regard the shepherd in days and years to come. David obviously thought a lot of Nathan despite the heavy message he brought. Paul, as we saw in another chapter, withstood Peter to his face over a doctrinal matter; yet in later years Peter writes about '*our beloved brother Paul*' and '*the wisdom given to him.*'[5] Paul still held Peter's love and respect.

Often in life I have heard men correctly oppose error but because of their manner of doing it (and God knows I have been guilty), their opponents are further away than before they started. Whether it be a father or mother dealing with a rebellious teenage child or an elder dealing with a wayward church member, they must try to hold the respect and love of the people they are dealing with. This is no easy matter and only the Holy Spirit can give us the help we need to keep the balance. May we not only be a Jonathan in someone's life but a Nathan.

Notes

1. 1 Corinthians 9.27
2. Charles R Swindoll: *Killing Giants, Pulling Thorns* (Multnomah Press 1978), p. 25.
3. *John 4.16*
4. *Galatians 6.1*
5. *2 Peter 3.15*

5: When even God is Silent

Dirk Bogard wrote a book which, quite frankly, I found one of the most moving descriptions of childhood I've ever read. It was its title that drew me in: *A Postillion Struck by Lightning*.

The 'postillion' was brought up in Sussex and then had to separate for schooling in Glasgow for a while. The boys in his school stuffed Dirk, the son of the art editor of *The Times*, down the toilet and flushed him because they reckoned he had a 'la-de-da' accent. Miserable and very unhappy being away from his parents whom he loved and who loved each other, Dirk wandered onto waste Glasgow tenement ground and in desperation set up a little boy's altar by a 'burn' (A Scottish stream), pleading with God to get him out of Glasgow. His description of his loneliness and what he felt was God's silence has caused me many a long thought.

What about the silence of God? Surely this problem must be among the most perplexing in the universe. In this book we have learned from the Scriptures that God speaks encouragement to his people by promises in his word. I have heard God speak in Jesus Christ: I've heard him speak messages of pardon and forgiveness, of hope beyond the grave, of the power for living. But sometimes God is silent regarding the perplexing problems of my immediate life. I ask him for reasons and he refuses to explain. It happened to Job.

Can You Love A Silent God?

The book of Job is a poem of tremendous power which is comparatively little read and even when it is read it is imperfectly understood. It abounds in allusions and long sequences of thought and its proverbial form is not easily grasped. No book needs to be exposed to the twentieth century more than the book of Job. The book is saying above all other things that a silent God is capable of inspiring affection and that man is capable of loving right simply because it is right and hating wrong because it is wrong even though he should not gain by it, but lose.

Job seemed to have lost. At the outset Job is put before us as the model of a perfect man. *'There is none like him on the earth, a blameless and upright man, one who fears God and shuns evil'*, said the Lord to Satan. Outwardly his conditions were large and prosperous and this provoked Satan to gibe, *'Does Job fear God for nothing?'*[2] God takes up the challenge and in his permissive will allows Satan to touch all Job has. Seven sons and three daughters are taken from him in a great storm, the Sabeans mount a raid and he loses all his livestock: seven thousand sheep, three thousand camels, one thousand oxen, five hundred female donkeys. His servants are also killed in the raid. Job's response was magnificent. He falls to the ground and says, 'The Lord gave, the Lord has taken away: blessed be the name of the Lord.'[3]

Then Job's health goes. He is smitten with a horrible disease that covers his entire body. He had

'some kind of acute dermatitis spreading everywhere and developing infections in which darkened (Job 30.28) and

peeling (30.30) skin and constantly emptying pustules (7.56)
would manifest the pruritus and purulence highlighted in
Job 2.7. Other symptoms may have been the results of
complications in the wake of such a severe malady:
anorexia: emaciation (19.20), fever (30.30b), fits of
depression (7.16; 30.15f), weeping (16.16a), sleeplessness,
such a putrid breath (19.17; cf 17.1), failing vision (16.16b),
rotting teeth (19.20) and haggard looks (2.12) are less direct
clues. They add up to a hideous picture of a man tortured by
degrading disfigurement and unendurable pain. [4]

Poor Job. He sat down among the ashes, the Mezbele; a
rubbish dump, burned once a month which grew to quite a
firm mound of earth serving a community's inhabitants as a
watchtower and on close oppressive evenings, as a place of
assembly because there is a current of air on the height.
There the children would play all day long and there the
forsaken would lie because their sickness would not allow
them back into the city or village. By day they would ask
alms of passers by and at night they would hide themselves
among the ashes which the sun had warmed.

'Curse God and die!' urges Job's wife, suggesting an
indirect way of committing suicide. But Job was no fair-
weather believer. Job rejects his wife's words with a fury,
but the illness continues and so does the silence of God.

Tunnel Light was an Oncoming Train

Ever been in such a position? Everything has caved in
around you and you have blessed God among your tears,
but still there are no indicators as to why it has all
happened. You think you see light at the end of the tunnel
but you discover the light to be an oncoming train!

Job's greatest trial was the arrival of his three friends

Eliphaz, Bildad and Zophar, generally reckoned to be from three different countries. Never did theologians bring less encouragement than these three: they believed that all miseries of life come from the hand of God and are sent to punish men for their sins. *'You must be a sinner Job!'* they all argue, *'Repent and you will be fine!'*

We must always watch the interpretations we put on the losses and sorrows of our friends when we visit them in order to encourage them in times of trouble. Job's comforters were certainly well intentioned but the result was that they increased his sorrows. Job's friends always remind me of my friend Noel Grant the evangelist who lay in hospital once. A 'friend' arrived to 'comfort' him with the immortal words, 'Noel, I had a relation who had what you have and she died!' Cold comfort, indeed!

Bystanders in sorrow are always of a more logical turn. It was not so easy for Job. He does not believe God is punishing his sins, he believes that he will be vindicated.[5] There are times when Job comes near to despair. He even gets so low he wishes he had never been born at all.[6] (It is worth pointing out that although some men may have despised the day of their natural birth I have never known anyone to despise the day of their new birth). The conflict of God's silence even makes him wonder at times if God is not acting like his enemy. It seems like that and Job says so and to our amazement God did not wipe him out for telling him how he felt. If we were to pray like Job in a church prayer meeting the elders would be having a word with us.

'Why do you hide your face,
And regard me as your enemy?
Will you frighten a leaf
Driven to and fro,
And will you pursue dry stubble?

. . . You put my feet in the stocks
And watch closely all my paths
And you inscribe a print for the soles of my feet.[7]

Job learned to trust a God he could no longer comprehend. God is good to the good and bad to the bad: that was the message of Job's friends but Job refused to have such a narrow view. His view was that God is sovereign and loving even though he may appear to be contradictory in the circumstances of our lives.

Please Take A Nature Ramble, Job!

When God at last spoke to Job, after a long and torturous silence, God pointed out to him that he had been in the dark because of certain knowledge which he lacked. God now supplied that knowledge. What an answer it was to Job and an answer none of us would have expected! Instead of explaining why Job has lost his health, his family and his business, God takes Job on a tour of the world God had created. God spoke of the sea, the rainstorm, the constellations, the dew, the ice, the snow, the clouds, the young ravens, the wild ox, the ostrich and the horse. Job is made to reflect on the mystery of instinct in the Ibex (or mountain goat) and how the young learn self-preservation. The Ibex is removed from men who supervise the breeding of their own flocks, these animals have their young unobserved and unsheltered.

'Can you make such animals, Job? Can you control them?', God is asking. Marvellously God is interpreting his omnipotence to Job. No words of explanation are given to explain why he has suffered. In fact an explanation is never given to Job during this lifetime. What Job needed was a true and real sight of God and then explanations became

unnecessary. *God alone, in himself, became his encouragement.*

> '*Does the hawk fly by your window,*
> *And spread its wings toward the south?*
> *Does the eagle mount up at your command,*
> *And make its nest on high?*'[8]

Job was overwhelmed by a new appreciation of the majesty and power of the God he was dealing with. '*What shall I answer to you? I lay my hand over my mouth*', he whispers. The silence of God is a mind-bending thing but the silence of Job is just as riveting.

One day every believer will come to see God face to face. When we see who and what God really is and truly get to know him we shall learn the enormous cheek of our puny demands during our earthly lifetime to have the key to our aims and purposes in our circumstances put into our hands. Yet the Lord's words to Job are not meant to humiliate him. They are meant to give Job a knowledge of himself and of God. Is it not one of the marvels of the book of Job that Job is brought to peace without even knowing all the facts of his case? Was he not thrust into trouble in order that his faith would be strengthened and that he would learn to love God *for God's sake?*

I always remember my good friend Peter Jackson the blind recording artist sitting at lunch in a friend's house. The friend asked him if he could handle soup. 'I eat by faith and not by sight!' replied Peter while we all rocked with laughter. Job was learning to live by it. As someone has said, '*Job did not say in the end "Now I see it all!" He never sees it all. He sees God*'

> '*I have heard of you by the hearing of the ear,*
> *But now my eye sees you,*

Therefore I abhor myself,
And repent in dust and ashes.'[9]

Authorised Biblical Hobbies

Someone may be reading these lines who desperately needs
encouragement in the perplexities of life: No pastor,
prelate, priest, parson, preacher, pope or person seems to be
able to give it to you. Right? Then, like David, you must
'encourage yourself in the Lord your God.'[10] I must, of
course, remind you that the Lord Jesus said that he was the
Way, the Truth and the Life and that no one comes to God
except by him. Without a hold on Christ there is no hold on
God at all. We must repent of our sins and trust in the Lord
Jesus as our Saviour. But that is only the start of the great
adventure of knowing God. We must learn to get to know
him better. The book of Job teaches us that one of the best
ways in which we can encourage ourselves in the Lord our
God is to take a walk in the woods or a stroll in the park! I
know that Evangelicals do not stress this very much and the
reason is that they do not read the book of Job often enough!
Evangelists and Bible teachers, pastors, and preachers
seldom talk much of gaining knowledge of God by gazing
on the world around us. Jesus talked a lot about it. The only
authorised hobbies in the Bible are botany and ornithology!
'Consider the lilies of the field: how they grow', he counselled,
'consider the birds of the air'. Job had no institutions to lean
on and no revealed knowledge to encourage him. He was
unsupported by tradition and contradicted by experience
but became the greatest believer in the Bible. How? By
looking at ordinary things around him with God. This
liberated him to live with joy.

Just this morning in my mail I received a letter from a
friend who had written to encourage me. He writes to me

often and always 'puts a match to my fire.' This morning's
letter read:

> 'I was thinking recently about the purpose of life,
> particularly if there is nothing "big" on, and most days are
> filled with humdrum activities. And then I read in
> Philippians about the goal of pleasing the Lord, and I
> realised that to do what I am doing, well, and to show a
> loving and caring attitude to everyone I meet, are ways that
> I can please the Lord – in even the little things of life.
>
> Perhaps if I was busier in "big things" I might have
> missed this.
>
> I pray that you too will continue towards that goal of
> trying to please him in the "big things" and in the "little
> things".'

Job had learned to please the Lord in the circumstances my
friend's letter highlights. Now life became something really
special for him.

'Go to my servant Job . . . and my servant Job shall pray
for you. For I will accept him, lest I deal with you according to
your folly: because you have not spoken to me what is right, as
my servant Job has,'[11] says God to Job's friends, '. . . and the
Lord restored Job's losses when he prayed for his friends.
Indeed the Lord gave Job twice as much as he had before.'[12]

God simply cannot be placed in a box of our own making.
Experience cannot be the only basis of faith in God because
experience is too limited. God must be God in the very
fullest meaning of that word. There is always one fact more
in every life that no one knows but God. Job learned to
accept this and in his acceptance difficulties became
opportunities. People who have suffered and come to accept
God's will have a ministry of encouragement, as Job
proved. People who have been through things are deeply

concerned about others. They have learned to accept God's will and to encourage others to do so, in the 'big' things and in the 'little'. Ask Job's friends!

'I will not forget the dying faces: the empty places,
They shall be filled again.
O voices moaning deep within me, cease.
But vain the word; vain, vain;
NOT IN FORGETTING LIETH PEACE.

He said, "I will withdraw me and be quiet,
Why meddle in life's riot,
Shut by my door to pain,
Desire, thou dost before me,
Thou shalt cease,"
But vain the word; vain, vain;
NOT IN ALOOFNESS LIETH PEACE.

He said, "I will accept the breaking sorrow,
Which God to-morrow,
Will to his son explain.
Then did the turmoil deep within him cease
Not vain the word, not vain:
FOR IN ACCEPTANCE LIETH PEACE.'

Amy CARMICHAEL

Notes

1. Job 1.8
2. Job 1.9
3. Job 1.21
4. Francis I Anderson: *Job: An Introduction and Commentary* (Tyndale OT Commentaries, General Editor: D J Wiseman IVP, 1976), pp. 91–92.

5. Job 13.16
6. Job 3.3
7. Job 13.25
8. Job 39.26
9. Job 42.5–6
10. Isaiah 30.6
11. Job 42.7–8
12. Job 42.10

6: Can I Encourage for the Sheer Reward?

So David had an encouraging friend in Jonathan, Moses in Aaron, Naomi in Ruth, Peter in John, Paul in Timothy and a host of other people in each other. Who, then, did the Lord Jesus have to encourage him?

It is a question I have pondered. God became a man in order to die for man. No-one, anywhere, ever came to accomplish a more important mission than the Son of God. From his childhood to his death I do not read of many people actually encouraging him to die for me. Most people seem to have done their best to dissuade him. His brothers and sisters were no help. Mary certainly pondered but Peter actually rebuked him and said, '*Far be it from you, Lord; this shall not happen to you.*'[1] Few seem to have understood. '*We were hoping*', said the two on the way to Emmaus after the Lord's death, '*that it was he who was going to redeem Israel*'[2] They obviously thought that the whole thing was a failure.

Wanted: A Pair of Sympathetic Ears

At our worst moments we have always found one person, if only one, to listen to our heart-breaking, or business-breaking, or career-breaking problems. Even if just to listen, most of us have found, somewhere, a pair of sympathetic ears. It should be emphasised that such a pair are not always easy to find.

Recently in America a man put an advertisement in a newspaper saying that he would listen to anyone talk, for thirty minutes without interrupting him for five US dollars a time. He got about forty telephone calls a day!

Perhaps you have a pair of sympathetic ears but lack advice on how to help people in trouble, particularly people who are emotionally or intellectually disturbed and who need help. Often in the work of God at the *Crescent Church* in Belfast we are deeply indebted to Dr D J C Dawson, a psychiatrist who is a Christian. His help and advice when dealing with people's problems has been invaluable. He once gave this advice on Christian counselling:

> '*The would-be counsellor should have some basic knowledge of human psychology, normal and abnormal. He must be a good listener, slow to interrupt, until he feels sure that he has something worthwhile to contribute, some helpful question to ask. The counsellor should be genuinely humble and receptive, with an objective approach to the problem under discussion, and he should avoid all well worn clichés, truisms and easy slick solutions. He is not there to sermonise or to moralise – certainly not till he has heard all that the enquirer has to say, and he must avoid a holier-than-thou attitude. Further, he should not show shocked surprise, disapproval or condemnation.*' (There, but for the grace of God, go I!)

While dealing objectively with the enquirer's problems, one should aim to establish rapport (an understanding relationship) and *empathy* (entering into the individual's feelings and fears).

If the sufferer talks freely you are fortunate, but do not

show impatience, should he or she be hesitant, slow or devious. Tears should not be discouraged, they relieve tension and may prove a useful pointer as to causative factors.

The counsellor is perhaps better equipped for his task, if he has experienced personal difficulties, problems, doubts and fears, even a sense of guilt and failure, perplexity and distress, but has come through to peace, both spiritually and emotionally.

One of the wonderful benefits of our Lord's incarnation is that '*because he himself has suffered being tempted, he is able to help those that are tempted*' (Hebrews 2.18 RSV). He knew tears, loneliness, conflict and agonising prayer, though always sinless and victorious.

The enquirer may be solely concerned with some point of doctrine or some sin, about which he is understandably distressed, and here, of course, the counsellor's ability to help will depend, not only on his biblical knowledge, but also on his spiritual maturity and insight, and the sincerity of his christian love and concern. (May I suggest that the approach should not be too academic and that the counsellor should be more concerned with the spirit than with the letter of the law, being careful *not to pressurise* the enquirer or to attempt to make up his mind for him. The Lord Jesus appears usually to have avoided doing so!)

The problem may be one for the application of common sense. If so, apply it and do not feel you have to be profound!

Again, the problem may be clearly a practical one, eg should he, a Christian, go into partnership with a non-Christian, join a Trade Union or become politically involved? While discussing the pros and cons, the final decision must be made by the enquirer.

The question of annulment of marriage or of divorce,

whichever is legally appropriate, may be raised by the enquirer. Medical or psychiatric aspects will require expert investigation and if the enquirer considers some definite action, legal advice will clearly be indicated. Usually the counsellor should avoid excessive dogmatism as to possible action, though he is of course justified in presenting christian teaching on the subject. Here again however, the final decision is not his!

We have not been created in water-tight compartments, but our various organs and functions, including our minds (thinking, feeling and willing), function interdependently (1 Corinthians 12. 14–26). *Physical illness* may be present with emotional and intellectual symptoms, and emotional illness is often accompanied by physical symptoms, eg. tension, tremor, sweating, palpitation, headache, disturbances of appetite and of sleep, indigestion, etc. Thus, should the enquirer not respond soon to discussion and advice, or should he continue to manifest physical symptoms, he should be advised to consult his doctor without undue delay.

A few practical suggestions:

1) Advise the enquirer to tell his story as fully as possible, not initially selecting what he considers to be most important. He should be completely frank as to his feelings and fears, his major worries or problems.

2) One should observe carefully, though unobtrusively, the enquirer, as to *facial expression* (anxious, apprehensive, tense or dull, miserable and hopeless); *general appearance, attitude and dress* (inert and dejected, tense and restless, fidgeting and tremulous, etc. Clean and tidy or careless in dress and dirty); *manner* (friendly and confiding; suspicious and hesitant; rude and aggressive); *speech* (Does he talk freely and coherently, or

is there a lack of spontaneity, so that answers are extracted with difficulty, tending to be brief or mono-syllabic?) This latter response suggests depression.

Medical help will be indicated:

1) If there is evidence of *severe depression* (with marked retardation or agitation), with hopelessness, not readily relieved by discussing his, or often her, problems, in one or two interviews. Any talk of *suicide* or of tiredness of life usually indicates some urgency! *Abnormal elation*, with no obvious cause, associated with marked pressure of talk, excitability, foolish jocularity or unprovoked anger and aggression, suggest some degree of mania.

2) If conversation is *vague and difficult to follow*, with perhaps, long pauses when the individual becomes 'lost'; also if the mood is rather *flat and colourless*, with episodes of incongruity, eg. foolish laughter when discussing quite serious matters, then one should suspect schizophrenia (usually youth to early middle life). If, in addition, there are definite hallucinations, eg. hearing one's own thoughts or external 'voices', also delusions of an absurd nature, the diagnosis becomes more certain. Such folk may express ideas of reference, misreading the innocent remarks or actions of others as having a specific reference to themselves, or ideas of influence (passivity feelings), eg. that others are controlling their thoughts or bodily functions through eg. radar, television, etc.

Do not argue with those who express psychotic symptoms, eg. delusions. Treat them with courtesy, but suggest to relatives that medical advice is indicated *now*.

3) If the conversation reveals *failing memory*, especially for recent events, if he is *repetitive* or *wandering*, *disorientated* as to the time, or failing to recognise close friends or relatives, or becomes lost in familiar

surroundings, then there is evidence of mental degener-
ation or confusion and medical advice is a *must*.

Guilt Many folk are burdened with feelings of guilt. Here
the gospel of forgiveness in Christ will have obvious value.

But, sometimes feelings of guilt appear to be genuinely
related to some past act of unkindness or dishonesty, etc.,
clearly indicating the need for apology or even restitution,
then the Christian counsellor may apply the teaching of
Matthew 5.23f. But, many over-scrupulous rigid and
obsessional perfectionists may worry intermittently for
years concerning some relative trivialities, which have done
no real harm to anyone, except the worrier. Here surely the
emphasis should be on God's wonderful and complete
forgiveness, available in Christ and Philippians 3.13 is
more appropriate! Some Christians appear never really to
have lost the burden from off their backs and here John
Bunyan's description in *Pilgrim's Progress* where Christian
came '*to a place somewhat ascending; and upon that place
stood a Cross . . . just as Christian came up with the Cross, his
burden loosed from off his shoulders, and fell from his back,
and began to tumble, and so continued to do, till it came to the
mouth of the sepulchre, where it fell in, and I saw it no more*',
contains the truth the burden-bearer needs most.

Finally, it is good practice to keep some notes on one's
more difficult cases, BUT UNDER LOCK AND KEY!
'Confidentiality is, of course absolutely essential.'

I judge Dr Dawson's advice to be most useful. May we
imbibe the truth of his advice as we listen to other people's
problems. Yet, when we think of our Saviour on earth very
few were sympathetic to him.

'*I have trodden the winepress alone, and from the peoples no
one was with me*',[3] say the Scriptures, speaking
prophetically. There was not one eye to pity, and not one

arm to save; even his disciples forsook him and fled. He had spoken and the world had been formed out of nothing. Making stars was but a small thing to him. The brightest of them are twenty thousand times as luminous as the sun. If the largest star were put with its middle where the sun is now, the whole of the Earth's path around the sun would lie inside it! Giant elliptical galaxies alone have ten million stars in them. '*And,*' says Genesis chapter one, '*He made the stars also.*' And, snowdrops and volcanoes, sparrows and oceans and you and me. When he died, there was no-one in all the universe or even in eternity itself to encourage him.

What kept him going through it all? When men were as the flies of summer, what kept him on the *Via Dolorosa?* Hugh Lindsay has a little phrase I hear him use sometimes: '*It was not,*' he will say, '*the nails which held him to the Cross.*' And, in the final analysis, it was not. '*Who for the joy that was set before him endured the Cross, despising the shame*',[4] wrote the writer to the Hebrews. That joy was his source of encouragement and his reward. That joy was to glorify his Father. That joy was the nail all hell could not loosen. He always did those things which pleased his Father. And so, in time, when Christians encourage others they must do so in order to glorify God. '*So you're going to China to convert the Chinese?*', said someone sarcastically to W C Burns. '*No*', he replied, '*I am going to China in order to glorify God.*' Christ's joy was also to have us with him. It was to bring '*many sons to glory.*'[5] His joy was to see, through his redemptive work at Calvary, rebels converted to supporters, sinners converted to saints, Charles Colsons[6] become prison evangelists, carrying the best news on the face of the earth. There is no deeper mystery. It is called the love of God.

The Taboo Word

Reward seems to be a taboo word with many Christians. I

remember discussing it with a friend and she kept insisting, '*But you only did what was your duty*'. In a way that was true in the circumstance preceding our discussion but reward for duty done is not something to be ashamed of. We unfortunately associate the word with a school prize day or standing on some Olympic games winner's block. We think of it as if it were a sneaking 'I-will-get-a-bigger-heavenly-mansion' thought!

The fact is that I may encourage someone in dire need of encouragement and no-one on earth may ever know about it except that person. But my heavenly father will know. Even when I pray in secret I am promised that my heavenly father will reward me 'openly'. Is that reward material gain? Is it public recognition of the success of a ministry of encouragement?

> '*We must not*', wrote C S Lewis, '*be troubled by unbelievers when they say that this promise of reward makes the christian life a mercenary affair. There are different kinds of reward. There is the reward which has no natural connection with the things you do to earn it and it is quite foreign to the desires that ought to accompany those things. Money is not the natural reward of love; that is why we call a man mercenary if he marries a woman for the sake of her money. But marriage is the proper reward for a real lover and he is not mercenary for desiring it : . . . the proper rewards are not simply tacked on to the activity for which they are given, but the activity itself in consummation*'.[7]

In the famous Old Testament story, Ruth would not leave her mother-in-law. She became a gleaner of corn for Naomi's sake and a lonely, miserable, back-breaking job it was. Did Ruth do this self-sacrificing work just to get a husband? Not at all. Yet God rewarded her with a wonderful husband who owned the field she gleaned in. The reward of Ruth's kindness to Naomi was when Ruth was able to lay her little baby boy, Obed, in Naomi's arms. I am not overstating my case. Notice what Naomi's friends in Bethlehem said:

> 'Then the women said to Naomi, "Blessed be the Lord who has not left you this day without a near kinsman; and may his name be famous in Israel! And may he be to you a restorer of life and a nourisher of your old age; for your daughter-in-law, who loves you, who is better to you than seven sons, has borne him.
>
> Then Naomi took the child and laid him on her bosom, and became a nurse to him. Also the local women gave him a name, saying, "There is a son born to Naomi." And they called his name Obed. He is the father of Jesse, the father of David'.[8]

Naomi had been grievously bereaved. She had lost her husband and her two sons. She had no grandchildren, no one to carry on the family name. Ruth knew it and set out to cheer her up, to stand by her, to go where she went, to live where she lived, to die where she died, to know the God Naomi knew. Her reward must have been sweet when the women of Bethlehem dubbed her son Naomi's son! Reward indeed.

A Definition of the Reward

> 'When then,' writes John Stott, 'is the "reward" which the heavenly Father gives the secret giver? It is neither public nor necessarily future. It is probably the only reward which genuine love wants when making a gift to the needy, namely to see the need relieved. When through his gifts the hungry

are fed, the naked clothed, the sick healed, the oppressed fed, the lost saved, the love which prompted the gift is satisfied. Such love (which is God's own love expressed through man) brings with it its own secret joys, and desires no other reward'.[9]

There may be near us this very day a christian leader who is being driven almost to despair by the difficulties of communicating the Gospel in these days. He may find that the young folk around him find the fantasy of Spielberg's 'E.T.' and his visit from an alien world exciting to watch and whose loneliness makes them cry. He may find that 'E.T.' moves them emotionally by a far greater degree than the true story of a baby boy born in a stable and far from his alien world: a baby who had come to die for our sins and who was raised for our justification – truth much stranger than fiction which seems to leave them cold. We can encourage that youth leader by our prayers and by our verbal, helpful support. We can lift up his hands in the battle for the minds of our young people and encourage him to preach and communicate the word of God, which, by the power of the Holy Spirit alone, can reach minds and hearts.

An old lady, now with her Lord, used to quote a Bible verse to me when as a young Christian reaching out in communicating the Gospel at public meetings I used to feel afraid and discouraged. *'Be not afraid of their faces, Derick'*,[10] she would say. Those words are alive in me even now. Such words have their reward.

Maybe near us is a disinterested young person who cares neither for God or man. He seems impossible to reach for the Lord Jesus. Let us not be afraid to speak to him of the needs of his soul. There is no calculating what a word of encouragement regarding God's love for him and the claims of the Gospel will do. Let me share an example of what I am talking about. It is really a story of a great reward for faithfulness.

The Drunkard who Started a Revival

One evening in the last century an immoral and drunken university student in Germany came upon a few Christians who were studying the Scriptures together. Their influence led to his conversion to Christ. He went to England and one morning shared his breakfast with a few orphan children who were hungry. Soon the few became many and he extended his kindness to giving them not just breakfast but all their meals, every day. A house purchased to accommodate the children soon became two houses, six houses, eight houses. Then it became an institution, the *'George Muller Houses for Orphans'*, sheltering two thousand children! Millions of pounds came Muller's way, sent by God in answer to his faith. The influence of George Muller's faith spread worldwide, he was received at the White House in Washington, he toured the world preaching the Gospel and millions, literally millions of lives were touched and blessed by this man of faith.

A record of God's dealings with Muller was published and a copy came into the hands of a Christian in Ireland, a man from County Antrim. He was so deeply influenced by Muller's faith in the living God he began to ask *'If God could do all this for Muller could he not do it for me?'* With three of his friends they prayed in the old schoolhouse in Kells, Co Antrim and asked God for a mighty blessing on Ireland. In 1859 it came. Twenty thousand people attended a prayer meeting in Belfast's Botanic Gardens. In Ballymena an eye witness told of five thousand people gathered in a quarry near the town to hear an old man, poorly dressed, a confirmed drunkard and converted just one week, preach the Gospel with tremendous power. The spiritual awakening spread everywhere in the island. It is said that in the whole of Ireland in 1859 upwards of one hundred thousand souls found the Lord Jesus as Saviour. If I remember right two of them were my great-grandparents. Through their influence, under God, the Christian message passed down through our family and, hence, you and I have met on this page! It all came because of the faithfulness of a few believers in Germany encouraging one another and their visitor with the Word of God.

We must, then, get this truth of reward in its right biblical perspective. We must with confidence live for the Lord Jesus despite all the problems and pressures. '*Therefore do not cast away your confidence*', says the writer to the Hebrews, '*which has great reward. For you have need of endurance, so that after you have done the will of God, you may receive the promise:*

"*For yet a little while, and he who is coming will come and will not tarry*" '.[11]

In the great choice Moses made to live for the Lord and not for himself, reward played a vital part. The Bible tells us that he chose '*Rather to suffer affliction with the people of God than to enjoy the passing pleasures of sin, esteeming the reproach of Christ greater riches than the treasures of Egypt; for he looked to the reward*'.[12]

Respect for God's reward is something we must always have. It takes faith to have that respect. Faith was a telescope to Moses. Through it he could see that earthly rank and greatness was a poor, vain, empty thing. Faith told him that sin's pleasures were transient. Faith told him that heaven's reward was far richer treasure than Egypt's. He respected faith's findings.

On Red Vegetable Soup

The word of God records for us that Esau, Jacob's brother, had no respect for the promise of spiritual blessing through his birthright. He despised it and sold it for some red vegetable soup. The promises of God inherent in his birthright were wonderful, but they were future. So Esau said, '*No thanks! I'm going to enjoy myself now. You, Jacob, can take the promises if you life.*' Esau had no respect for God's reward and he ended up a tearful, heart-broken, sorrowing man.[13]

For selling his birthright Esau got the nickname of Edom, which means 'Red', for it was red soup he bought at the cost of his birthright. All his followers were called Edomites, the greatest of whom was Herod. '*Beware*', said Jesus to his disciples, '*of the leaven of Herod*'. The leaven of the Pharisees was hypocrisy but what was the leaven of Herod? Herod was the man who, knowing full well that the Scriptures showed the new King, the Messiah would be born in Bethlehem, deliberately determined to kill him. Why? Because Edomites choose to have their portion now rather than know God's reward later. They have absolutely no respect for the recompense of God's reward. Wait for Messiah to come and for Israel to be raised to the head of the nations? Not Herod!

I wonder, in the light of all this, how we are in our hearts? Are we like Edom or like Moses? Do we compromise our faith because the coming of our Lord Jesus seems to tarry? Do we choose earthly treasure which worms and rust and thieves and inflation and devaluation wreck and ruin or heavenly treasure which cannot know decay in any form? Do we listen to the culture and society around us and make, as Christians, unholy alliances with the weird and false religion so long as our appetites are fed to the full now? Let us rather be like Moses who respected God's promises and *'by faith . . . forsook Egypt not fearing the wrath of the King; for he endured, as seeing him who is invisible.'*[14]

Can I encourage for the sheer reward? I would be a very foolish Christian if I didn't. Christians should treat reward with great respect.

Notes

1. Matthew 16.22
2. Luke 24.21
3. Isaiah 63.3
4. Hebrews 12.2
5. Hebrews 2.10
6. Special Counsel to Richard M Nixon before and during the Watergate scandal.
7. *They Asked for a Paper* (Bles, 1962), p. 108.
8. Ruth 4.14–17
9. *Christian Counter Culture* (IVP, 1978), p. 132.
10. Jeremiah 1.8
11. Hebrews 10.35
12. Hebrews 11.26
13. Hebrews 12.17
14. Hebrews 11.27

7: 'A Divot to my Draigon'[1]

'I used to fly a kite as a laddie', said my encouraging Scots friend Mr Willie McClachlan. One day he was out trying to get his kite to lift into the air and it was flying most erratically and then diving to earth and breaking the bow. 'What you need', said a passer by, 'Is a divot to your draigon, sonny.'

'A *what?*' asked Willie.

'A divot to your draigon!' he replied.

'The man leaned down and took up a small clod of earth and grass and tied it to my kite string. Away she soared, perfectly! The divot gave the kite weight and balance.'

When Willie told me that story it reminded me of part of a poem on the power of words. The thought behind these lines is a most serious one.

> *'Boys flying kites haul in their white winged birds*
> *You can't do that when you're flying words.'*

Words, once uttered, can never be retrieved. The lady implored of the preacher what she should do about all the words which she had used to slander people in her village before her conversion to Christ. 'Go', said the preacher, 'and get some down[2] and one night put some at the door of every household you have slandered.' She did so and went back to ask the preacher what to do next. 'Go and gather them all up,' he said. When she returned the down had scattered in the wind forever. She got the point.

A suicide's body was found floating in a river and a note was written on her person. The note had only two words written on it: '*They said.*' Do we realise what a word from our tongues can do? It can wreck a local church, mar a child for life, disrupt the harmony of a business office and destroy a marriage. I know what I am writing of: I very nearly destroyed a marriage.

The Marriage I Nearly Wrecked

A friend of mine, a long time ago, a lovely Christian girl was keeping company with a young chap I also knew. She later married him and I thought she was happy until one day she asked me to come and see her. She was ill and very depressed. 'Do you remember what you said about my relationship with my husband?' she asked. 'No, I don't,' I innocently and truthfully replied.

'Well, one day when I went out with him first you said to someone else that you didn't think he suited me. What you said was passed on to me and again and again I think of your words and wonder if I was right to marry him.'

What a bombshell! A glib statement in private to someone had become a haunting nightmare in the teeth of a young wife's depression. I apologised because no one could have been more wrong about the suitability of her husband than I had been. No-one ever had a better husband and, thank God, the depression lifted and that relationship has led to a lot of blessing for a lot of people. Oh! that I had had a divot to my draigon!

'*If anyone does not stumble in word, he is a perfect man, able also to bridle the whole body,*' wrote James. '*The tongue is a little member and boasts great things. See how great a forest a little fire kindles!*

And the tongue is a fire, a world of iniquity. The tongue is so set among our members that it defiles the whole body and sets on fire the course of nature: and is set on fire by hell.'

I have seen a killer whale trained by a man who rode past me on its back. I have seen tigers obey a trainer's whim. I have even seen parrots ride on roller skates! *'But the tongue can no man tame,'* says God's word. Only the Lord can control a person's tongue by the power of the Holy Spirit until it speaks good, wholesome, edifying, Christ-exalting words. And they are more quality-words than quantity-words. *'I would rather speak five words with my understanding that I may teach others also,'* wrote Paul, *'than ten thousand words in an unknown tongue.'*

Solomon, once the wisest man in all the earth, wrote a lot of things about the power and influence of speech both as to how it could be used for positive encouragement to the people around us or how it unfortunately can be used to devastate lives. One of the latter kind is the immoral woman's speech. Such woman's words drew Solomon from being a wise and mighty leader to becoming an effeminate fool in a very, very, short space of time. Will we learn from God's word by warning or will we learn from bitter experience?

'My son pay attention to my wisdom . . .
The lips of an immoral woman drip honey,
And her mouth is smoother than oil;
But in the end she is as bitter as wormwood
Sharp as a two-edged sword,
Her feet go down to death,
Her steps lay hold of hell.'[4]

In our day and generation such women exist by the million and we have been warned. But Solomon speaks of another kind of speech: it is the speech of a contentious woman, a woman given to quarrelling and strife. She is, as those who know her will tell you, a pain in the neck and rottenness to your bones.

'*It is better to dwell in the corner of a housetop than in a house shared with a contentious woman,*'[5] writes Solomon, and then seems to think again and declares, '*It is better to dwell in the desert*'[6] than live with her! '*A continual dripping on a very rainy day and a contentious woman are alike: whoever restrains her, restrains the wind and grasps oil with his right hand!*'[7] It sounds as if Solomon knew her well!

Very different is the woman whose heart the Lord has touched. 'The heart of her husband safely trusts her . . . she opens her mouth with wisdom and on her tongue is the law of kindness.'[8]

A Kiss! A Jewel! The Delight of Kings!

Speech. If only we could see what an encouraging word of kindness could do we would pour out thousands of them daily. Solomon realised, under the inspiration of the Spirit, what such words could do: '*Anxiety in the heart of a man causes depression, but a good word makes it glad.*'[9] '*He who gives the right answer kisses the lips.*'[10] '*There is gold and a multitude of rubies but the lips of knowledge are a precious jewel.*'[11] '*The words of a man's mouth are deep waters, the well spring of wisdom is a flowing brook.*'[12] '*Death and life are in the power of the tongue.*'[13] '*Righteous lips are the delight of kings and they love him who speaks what is right.*'[14]

Gladness! A kiss! A jewel! Deep waters! Life! The delight of kings! So God's word describes the power and value of our words if they are right. Let's choose them well.

In any one day we meet a lot of people and those of us who are believers must constantly ask the Lord to give us the right word for the people we meet. Let us trace a husband and wife's progress through any one day, at least in a few of the situations they face. Let us look at the day through a wife's eyes. Let her try this on her husband first thing in the morning, all things being equal:

'That was a lovely thing you said to the children at tea yesterday, dear.' He will be waiting for a scolding but what a surprise if he finds you are commending him for something kind he said yesterday! After picking himself up from the floor, following the experience of the nearly fainting, he will have a great day! Thirteen little words, but what a glad heart you will have made. Put a divot to your draigon!

As you see your husband off and struggle to get your children to school through the cries of *'Where's my "this"?'* and *'Where's my "that"!'* and *'No! I'm not wearing it!'* and your house is still strewn with toys and model kits and comics and dolls at 8.25 am which at 9.30 pm the night before you cleaned up before you were lowered into bed: whisper *'I love you'* in their ears before they depart. You may not feel like this, *but do it.* You will never be able to calculate what those three little words do in a childs heart. Put a divot to your draigon!

A fellow Christian, Joe Morrow, once told me that he had been working in his garden. His children were running about like any other children (half wrecking the place!), and he got really annoyed with them. Suddenly the phone rang. The subsequent conversation informed Joe that a little boy had just fallen off a cliff while on holiday and had been killed. The little boy's father had phoned Joe to tell him what had happened.

Joe went out into the garden again but was a different father now. 'You can wreck the garden if you like,' he told

his children, 'I am only too glad you are alive!' Few parents
would disagree with the sentiment he expressed that sad
afternoon. Somehow the frolics and fun of his little boy and
girl didn't annoy him so much. *Tell your children that you
love them!* They just might not come back this afternoon.
Put a divot to your draigon!

And now all the house is cleared and you have the
shopping to do. Ah! shopping. In heaven, praise the Lord,
there will be no more supermarket check-out queues. Or,
maybe I write to someone going out tomorrow morning to
an African or an Asian market – oh! the bargaining! Be
patient. Speak a kind word to the assistants or stall owners.
Don't make it bland like a girl who issued an airline ticket
to a doctor I know; 'Have a good day!' she said as he
departed. 'I'm flying to my father's funeral,' he replied. She
had nothing to say to that. Let's not be bland but at the
same time let us remember that a *'God bless!'* is a rare
occurrence to hear these days. Put a divot to your draigon as
you shop!

So, you meet with others at some function or other
tomorrow. They start to whisper gossip about someone you
know. Solomon reminds you that though gossip is attractive
and *'the words of a tale bearer are like tasty trifles . . . they go
down into the innmost body,'*[15] he also warns that *'a whisper
separates the best of friends.'*[16] Draw a curtain of silence
around you in such circumstances. Meddle with it and you
will be like one *'who takes a dog by the ears.'*[17] If asked,
speak of the good you know of in your friend and say no
more. May the law of kindness rule your tongue all day,
lady! Only the Holy Spirit can do that in you from a heart
and life which has been born again. Let the fear of the Lord
be in your heart for *'Charm is deceitful and beauty is vain,
but a woman who fears the Lord, she shall be praised.'*[18] It is
worth remembering that *'As a ring of gold in a swines snout,*

so is a beautiful woman who lacks discretion.'[19]

And we men, how about our tongue? That christian girl we loved and wooed and wept for: what we have won by prayer, do we wear with praise? *'Her husband also, and he praises her.'*[20] Praise from a husband is sometimes rarer than we think. How about a 'that was a delicious breakfast, Mary' tomorrow morning? As Mary picks herself up from fainting on the floor tell her that you will be taking her out for dinner tomorrow night and that a baby sitter has been arranged (Do that tonight after finishing this chapter!) See how such words will change her day. Marriage works both ways and kind actions beget kind actions.

And how about this for tomorrow's motto: *'I am determined, no matter what, to speak a kindly word to every man, woman and child who crosses my path for any length of time today.'* Perhaps that may mean a word of counsel to a friend who desperately needs it. We can be as oil and perfume to someone's heart today. How? Ask Solomon: *'Ointment and perfume delight the heart; so a man's counsel is sweet to his friend.'*[21]

If, men, our hearts know, love and trust the Lord Jesus, the people we do business with will notice it whether those people be hard-headed 'giants' of industry and commerce or our own employees; we will no more be able to hide the Lord Jesus in our lives than a fellow can hide the fact that he is in love. How? By the magazines we don't look at as well as the ones we do look at: by the alcohol we refuse, for, *'Wine is a mocker, intoxicating drink arouses brawling and whoever is led astray by it is not wise;'*[22] by the videos we would not take should they be for nothing; for the bribes we refuse, for *'the King establishes the land by justice but he who receives bribes overthrows it.'*[23]

Are we only to be known by the things we refuse? Certainly not. It is *who we are* in our hearts that really counts. *'How does your head lie, Sir Walter?'* said his executioner. *'It matters not where my head lies, now,'* he replied, *'it is where the heart lies that counts.'*

A man, according to Scripture, is the head of his household. If he cares for his wife, takes time to counsel, love and train his children, always, in his heart, seeking to put God first, there will be blessing. Solomon wrote, *'The righteous man walks in his integrity: his children are blessed after him.'*[24] When we come home at night, men, will the sound of our footfall be welcome? Would we not be happy if in some day far distant our son or daughter were to turn with eager eye to the young men and women of their generation and say, with gladness, *'My dad used to say . . .?'* Miserable should we be if they can remember nothing that was worth repeating.

Let us all weigh our words carefully before we speak them because words, like an Irish mile, go a long, long, way. Put a divot to your draigon!

It is a fact that a discouraging word to someone will stay in the mind much longer than an encouraging word. As a preacher I know that should fifty people tell me they enjoyed a message I had given from the Lord and one person should say the word given was dreadful I should remember that discouraging word.

The story is told of the visiting preacher who was shaking hands with the congregation as they filed out at the close of his message. Along came a little man in a grey coat and shaking hands with the preacher he said, 'You were absolutely hopeless.' The little man slipped away out of a side door, went up the side of the church building and came in the top side door and rejoined the congregation still filing out.

He reached the preacher again and shaking hands with him said: 'You read your notes a lot and they weren't worth reading!' The little man slipped away out the side door and sure as daylight appeared again at the top side door, rejoined the still filing out congregation and said: 'We hope you don't come back again.'

'I've enjoyed my visit,' said the visiting preacher to the resident one after everyone had gone, 'but who is the little man in the grey coat?'

'Ah!' was the reply. 'Don't worry about him – he is a bit simple in the mind, he only repeats what he hears everyone else saying!'

The Glorious 283

John Pollock in his widely acclaimed biography of the man who led the campaign against slavery in England, William Wilberforce, tells of the great debate in the House of Commons on the Second Reading of the Bill for the abolition of the Slave Trade:

'The House divided: Ayes, 283, Noes, 16, majority for the aboliton, 267, a surprisingly overwhelming vote.'

'No one expected this great question to be carried with so high a hand,' wrote Harrowby's brother, one of the ayes. 'No one is more surprised than Wilberforce himself. He attributes it to the immediate interposition of Providence! The lights still burned at 4 Palace Yard where friends flocked in, including poor William Smith who had lost his seat for Norwich and had listened from the gallery.

. . . William Smith called out that they should name the sixteen miscreants: he had four already. Wilberforce looked up from the floor, where he was on one knee writing at a table as he often did, and said, "Never mind the miserable 16, let us think of our glorious 283".'[25]

We could well do with Wilberforce's spirit when facing little men in grey coats! Let us make sure that when we speak we are always amongst those who could be called 'glorious'. Let's put a divot to our draigon!

Notes

1. A *'draigon'* in broad Scots means a Kite.
2. First feathers of young birds. These are very soft and light.
3. James 3.5–6
4. Proverbs 5.1–4
5. Proverbs 21.9
6. Proverbs 21.19
7. Proverbs 27.15
8. Proverbs 31.26
9. Proverbs 12.25
10. Proverbs 24.26
11. Proverbs 20.15
12. Proverbs 18.4
13. Proverbs 18.21
14. Proverbs 16.13
15. Proverbs 18.6–8
16. Proverbs 16.28
17. Proverbs 26.17
18. Proverbs 31.30
19. Proverbs 11.22
20. Proverbs 31.28
21. Proverbs 27.9 (NASB)
22. Proverbs 20.1
23. Proverbs 29.4
24. Proverbs 20.7
25. John Pollock, *Wilberforce* (Lion Publishing; First Published by Constable & Company Limited, 1977) p. 212

8: What is God Like?

Robert Burns lived in Ayrshire in Scotland. The village of Alloway will always be associated with that amazing ploughman poet whose writing captured the heart of a nation. Recently I was led by God to preach in that beautiful district by the river Doon. A local church in nearby Ayr, full of kindly, enthusiastic Christians, asked me to preach and teach God's word amongst them over a period of six months. The only problem was, they asked me to preach on the first thirty-nine chapters of the book of Isaiah.

Why was this a problem? Read the first thirty-nine chapters of Isaiah! Israel had wandered far away from the Lord. God was angry with them and jealous for them so that Isaiah is sent to warn them that they are going to be sent into exile. For thirty-nine chapters Isaiah thundered, cajoled, pleaded with God's people to repent. When applying these amazing passages of scripture to my Scottish congregation I had to plead with them to remember that I had not come over from Ireland to be forever scolding them, but that it was God's word we were dealing with, not mine. We were all humbled by it. I do not exaggerate when I say that week-end by week-end God's Spirit did something in those services that none of us will ever forget.

What James Galway is to the flute, what Tolstoy is to literature, what Rembrandt is in the world of painting,

Isaiah is among the prophets. His incomparable contribution stands at the head of the seventeen prophetical books of the Bible.

Isaiah's writing has a colour, a profusion of imagery, a vividness of description and such amazing variety that it is quite a breathtaking book to read. A well-educated man and a friend of kings, historiographer at the Judean Court, Isaiah was married and continued in his ministry for about sixty years. Bold, patriotic, spiritual and tender, Isaiah was at once the greatest romantic and the greatest realist of his day.

At chapter 40 of his book, Isaiah's theme changes and from then until the sixty-sixth chapter we have the greatest Messianic poem in the Bible. At the very centre of this poem is the famous fifty-third chapter, and at the exact grammatical centre of this famous chapter is the immortal line which speaks of our lovely Lord Jesus: *'He was led as a lamb to the slaughter.'* Isaiah put *'the lamb'* at the centre and that is where he must always be placed. God has made the Lord Jesus the very centre of history, prophecy and redemption. No wonder Isaiah's writings were such a blessing!

On Duncan's T-shirt

Isaiah's message was not localised for his day but it is the dynamic, thrilling message needed for the day in which we live right now. The christian church is not all it should be: compromise, liberal theology, denial of great scriptural truths, wordliness, apathy, have all wreaked havoc across the life of the church of Christ. False gods have been flirted with. The church has known failure. You and I have sinned and have known the chastening of the Lord because when a person becomes a Christian he cannot do as he likes. I noticed recently in a congregation of people in mid Scotland a huge barrel-chested man called Duncan Donaldson sitting listening. He had a T-shirt on and emblazoned across the T-shirt in blue lettering on a white background were the words, *'Under new management!'* Duncan, formerly known as 'The Wild Man of Airdrie', was a new man in Christ. His message was clear. Unfortunately Christians have not always obeyed the new management and they have suffered for it.

We often bring a lot of sorrow upon ourselves. We neglect to read God's word and to spend time in prayer, we do not witness for the Lord Jesus as we should. Spiritual dry-rot gets into our lives. Like a spore of natural dry-rot which can sit on a surface for years waiting for the right conditions to arise in order to suddenly sprout and spread, so, once-cherished sins which we boasted were gone suddenly sprout anew because they have just been waiting for the right conditions to come around again. Illness and financial pressure, rebellion of children, divisions in the church, hasty words, wrong decisions; I find that God's people, never to speak of others, are in dire need of comfort. Is the encouragement of God's comfort available to his erring people?

'Comfort, yes, comfort my people!', says God through his servant Isaiah. *'Speak comfort to Jerusalem, and cry out to her, that her warfare is ended that her iniquity is pardoned: for she has received from the Lord's hand double for all her sins. The voice of one crying in the wilderness: "Prepare the way of the Lord; make straight in the desert a highway for our God. Every valley shall be exalted, and every mountain and hill shall be made low; the crooked places shall be made straight, and the rough places smooth; the glory of the Lord shall be revealed and all flesh shall see it together: for the*

mouth of the Lord has spoken" '.[1]

Comfort from God! The people had been exiled to Babylon. Mountains, valleys and long crooked and rugged roads lay between them and home. They felt they would never know the glory of the Lord again nor ever see their own homes. They were wrong. *'Crooked places shall be made straight and rough places smooth,'* says God through Isaiah. God specialises in things thought impossible. The thirty days journey across desert terrain between Babylon and Israel, the proud monarchy which held the people of God captive: all seemed too impossible to overcome. But nothing is impossible with God. *'Comfort them,'* says God to his prophet.

We have discussed in this book the fact that God uses all kinds of people to encourage and comfort his people. We have seen that Job got a new vision and realisation of God which far surpassed the help and encouragement of his friends: now we shall see that God wants all of his people to realise what he is like, every single one of them. Isaiah goes out to the people of God with God's message of comfort – but how does he convey such a message? *He shows them God.*

'Behold your God!', he cries. What, then is God like? We hear a lot about what God does. He *'has measured the waters in the hollow of his hands . . . and calculated the dust of the earth in a measure,'* notes Isaiah. To him *'the nations are as a drop in a bucket and are counted as the small dust on the balance.'* He flings stars into being and *'he calls them all by name.'* But what is he like?

'He will feed his flock like a shepherd: he will gather the lambs with his arm, and carry them in his bosom, and gently lead those that are with young'.[2]

He is no Hireling

I just love the image of the Lord as a shepherd in the midst of the tremendous imagery of Isaiah 40. There is no more encouraging thought. It reminds me of a walk I had one day in the Manchester Art Gallery. Musing on the paintings I was suddenly 'arrested' by a large canvas called *The Hireling* by Holman Hunt. In a glass case below, a letter from Holman Hunt to the curator of art at the gallery explained what he was trying to say in his painting. The artist's explanation transformed the meaning of the painting for me. Let me tell you about it, simply.

On a bank, in the painting, sat a young man in shepherd's garb. He was a hireling brought in for a few pennies to stay with the flock for a very short time. His heart was not in the work: he could not have cared less about the sheep. As he sits on a bank he is talking to a girl about a death head moth which he has in his hand, an object of superstition in England. While the hireling and the girl surmise what omen the moth has brought, two of the sheep are already in the cornfield eating the corn. They are as good as dead for if sheep eat corn they get blown stomachs and die. This image the artist explained, was like pastors who claim to be shepherds of Christ's flock who speculate on mere superstition in their pulpits, whilst their flock are going headlong to perdition and being given the wrong food all the time.

The rest of the flock in the painting are all, meanwhile, standing, apart from two sheep who are sick and are lying down. The reason why the rest of the flock are standing is because sheep will only normally lie down when they feel secure and safe. This flock feel neither.

There on the other side of the bank on which the hireling and the girl are sitting are the little yellow marshmallow flowers. Marshmallow flowers only grow where the ground is marshy and wet. The hireling had got his flock on the wrong feeding ground and they will all develop foot rot.

The background for this most moving painting is, of course, the words used by the Lord Jesus to describe himself. Just as Isaiah describes the almighty God as a shepherd, so the Lord Jesus describes himself, showing further, of course, his deity.

> *'I am the good shepherd',* he said, *'The good shepherd gives his life for his sheep. But he who is a hireling and not the shepherd, one who does not own the sheep, sees the wolf coming and leaves the sheep and flees; and the wolf catches the sheep and scatters them. The hireling flees because he is a hireling and does not care about the sheep. I am the good shepherd: and I know my sheep and am known by my own.'*[3]

It is most encouraging to know by experience that the Lord is no hireling. *'He will gather his lambs with his arm and carry them in his bosom, and gently lead those who are with young',* says Isaiah. His food is his word. The comforter is the Holy Spirit, dwelling within his flock, poured like oil upon their heads, calming them. His commitment to his flock is beyond compare. As F. B. Meyer put it: Gloom? *'Fear not, I am with you.'* Enemies? *'Be not dismayed for I am your God.'* Heart and flesh fail? *'I will strengthen you.'* Insurmountable difficulties? *'I will help you.'* Stumbling? *'I will uphold you with the right hand of my righteousness.'*

Impossible things become possible when the Lord is your shepherd. God had severely chastened his people Israel by allowing them to be taken into captivity in Babylon but now he is about to move to deliver them according to Isaiah's encouraging word. How could it happen? It happened through a heathen monarch.

Cyrus, the chieftain of an obscure Persian tribe became leader to two tribes and then swept in conquest from the frontier of India to the Aegean. God was seeing to it that he did. Bit by bit, unknown to Cyrus, God led him to the very gates of Babylon where he demanded the recognition of his supremacy. Babylon held out against Cyrus' seige for many long and difficult months. But one night Belshszzar made a feast to a thousand of his lords and suddenly, in the midst of their revelry as they drank out of the sacred cups plundered from Jerusalem's temple, a mystic hand on the wall decreed that the Medes and Persians were about to take over.

That night Cyrus diverted the mighty river that crossed the city of Babylon into a resevoir which had been set aside for water storage. Then his troops marched up the oozy channel left by the river and overthrew Babylon. Daniel soon acquainted Cyrus with the history of his people, Israel, and Cyrus let them go free.

So is this shepherd still. He shapes the future of our lives. Was it not a clerical error that sent Corrie Ten Boom out of the gates of the Ravensbruck concentration camp instead of to the gas chamber? Whose hand guided that German typist? Was it not the same hand which drew Corrie's sister Betsie, through death, to himself for his own purposes in the camp after uttering those haunting words that '*there is no pit so deep that Christ is not deeper still?*' Does not Hebrews chapter eleven teach us that God delivers some of his people from their foes and some of his people to their foes?[4]

The Woman who Demolished Slavery

I walked recently with my good friend Val English on the estate of the great American leader George Washington. Val has for years been one who has constantly helped me on bright days as well as dark ones. That particular afternoon we saw together that ominous little sign by the carefully manicured lawns which read *'To the slave quarters'*. It caused me to think deeply. What got rid of the despicable slave trade that even George Washington indulged in? Even Washington acted benevolently in comparison with those so ably described by Alex Hayley in his epic book *Roots* which became such an international television sensation and altered the way millions of Americans viewed themselves. What finally rooted the slave trade of North America out?

'The death knell of the slave trade was wrung by a woman's hand', wrote the man who probably hated the slave trade most, Dr David Livingstone. The woman's hand he spoke of was that of Harriet Beecher Stowe. Harriet wrote a book called *Uncle Tom's Cabin*. Her book wove into its story the sheer ugliness of the slave trade in such a way that it slowly saturated the conscience of white America until white Americans just had to abolish the practice. What the guns of the Civil War could not do, Harriet did. What inspired her? The Word of God which her parents had taught her. Read *Uncle Tom's Cabin* and you will see just how deeply the scriptures influenced Harriet. The good shepherd guided a woman's pen to free a people.

I began this chapter with Robert Burns. Let me end with him. On January 26, 1796 Burns wrote to a friend in what proved to be one of his last letters:

> *'Dear Mr Clarke,*
> *Still, still the victim of affliction. Were you to see the emaciated figure who now holds the pen to you, you would not know your old friend. Whether I shall ever get about again is only known to him, the great unknown, whose creature I am. Alas, Clarke, I begin to fear the worst.'*

Poor Rabbie! God seems to him to be *the great unknown*. Is that what God is like? Isaiah certainly does not think so. When Isaiah wrote that God smooths rough places, turns mountains into valleys, makes crooked ways straight he spoke the truth. When he said our God was a shepherd, that is exactly what he is like. He is a shepherd who can be known, he is no hireling. All the time the shepherd is silently planning for his flock in love. Nothing will go amiss from his care. He can take a baby's tears, as he did Moses' and on such a tiny thing as a tear, save a nation. This shepherd can reach anywhere and use anything for the good of his flock.

Does that not encourage you, Christian? Look up, there he is in front of you. Though you may be lonely, you are never alone. Tell somebody about your Lord, to-day. It may encourage them to come to know him too.

Notes

1. Isaiah 40.1–5
2. Isaiah 40.11
3. John 10.11–14
4. Hebrews 11.32–40

9: Encouragement Takes Time

She was utterly bereaved. Seldom in my life have I witnessed a woman who missed her husband so deeply. In over a year of widowhood she had often turned the thought of suicide over in her mind.

'I suppose your friends have all had plenty of advice for you?' I asked, gently.

'Of course!', she replied, 'they all tell me to telephone them if I feel lonely. I do and one by one they all tell me that they must hurry because they have a cake in the oven!'

We all have our own cakes in the oven. Excuses pour into our heads when we are faced with taking extra time with someone in order to encourage her. The christian church is full of the expression 'Hello! How are you?' at its gatherings. I often wonder if I honestly told these hello-how-are-you folk just how I really was, would they take fifteen minutes to listen, let alone five? Generally you find the cake will get more attention than you will.

Encouragement is a time-consuming ministry. My good friend Jean Wilson is well known as the Secretary of the British Christian Booksellers Convention. This convention draws Christian booksellers and publishers together from around the world in order to encourage them in their work. Recently Jean asked me to attend this Convention and I was amazed when she told me that it had taken, with the help of her small staff, nine hundred hours of telephoning to set up the Convention! It even takes time to encourage Christian booksellers!

Give Them Your Time

When our first child was born a friend sent a card with words that deeply affected us. It read *'The most precious commodity you can give to your child is your time'*. Thinking about it we tried to take the word to heart and busy days of deadly serious christian work were mixed with walks in the Tipperary Woods, stickleback fishing, romps to the top of many a hill to get a kite airborne, Lego building and other glorious escapades. It was not always easy to switch from feeding hungry hearts with God's word in a city famous for its bombs and bullets to the needs of small children who want your time *now!* It never will be easy for any parent no matter where they might live. We must learn that though electronic toys may fascinate and gobs of money spent on children at Christmas or any other time may seem to please them, children will not ultimately judge us by such things. Did we or did we not spend time with them? This question will weigh heavily in their judgement of us.

Recently a gracious christian couple talked to me at their dining-room table. The lady had been a preacher's daughter and now, in middle age, bitterly regretted the fact that her father had not spent much time with her.

'What is your earliest recollection?', I asked.

'I was five', she said, 'and I remember my father on the railway station going off to preach and his having to take me into a shop to pacify me. I had no real childhood. I can never remember my father at home on one single Christmas morning during my childhood.'

The Bible certainly does teach that if any man leaves his

parents or property, his wife and children for the Gospel's sake he will be rewarded. But does this imply that he must not spend time with his mother or father, his land, his wife or his child? Abraham left all for God but he certainly did not neglect to spend time with Isaac. No boy had closer attention from a father who travelled most of his life for God over vast wildernesses. Abraham even had a huge feast arranged for his son to celebrate his weaning![1] Look at the interest he took to ensure that Isaac found a good wife.

Didn't the Lord Jesus spend thirty years with his mother and father? No one ever gave more for God's Gospel than Jesus did. He was God and it was his Gospel, and yet in agony on Calvary he saw to it that his mother had provision for the rest of her days.

Very often over-attendance at church services as much as under-attendance can have a very bad effect upon children. Does the New Testament demand that Christians attend services of the church every night of the week? If so could somebody, somewhere tell me where the demand is? I believe 'meetingitis' is a disease and many a heart-broken child has been marred for life with bitterness because of parents who had no time to knock off and go for a walk in the park, a swim in the pool, a putter in a motor boat, a swing on a swing, a see-saw on a see-saw or spend an evening by the fire with THEIR CHILD. For a parent not to spend time with their children is a *sin*. How on earth can a child be brought up in the nurture and admonition of the Lord if a mother and father are forever working or forever going to meetings? God put families together before he put churches together. Local church activities are not a substitute for healthy, legitimate family exercise, games, projects, holidays etc.

The Television Trance

One thing is certain. If we do not spend vital time with our children, other communicators will see to it that our children have plenty of their time. In Britain alone two children in every three are watching television between three to five hours a day. That is twenty-one to thirty-five hours a week. In the United States pre-school children constitute the largest television audience and their weekly average viewing time is at least thirty hours. By the age of seventeen the average American child has logged fifteen thousand hours watching television – the equivalent of almost two years day and night. Television encourages passivity and diminishes creativity. And it disrupts natural family life. Worst of all, it induces what has been called 'the television trance'. It has not merely blurred the distinctions between the real and unreal for steady viewers, but ... by doing so it has dulled their sensitivities to real events.'

Are we going to allow our children to live life or simply sit and watch it? Television will not go away so it is up to us to be selective as to what they watch. If we are going to restrict their viewing than I would encourage – urge – parents to provide alternatives for them; things to do, places to go, and that means that parents must get up and get involved with their children.

> It is not hard to make a child's heart glad,
> Often a little thing will please, will ease,
> A tear-filled afternoon,
> A walk, a ride across the park,
> A story read, a small surprise,
> A 'let's pretend', will soon,
> Have a child's heart glad.

Father, busy in your office plush,
Rushing around so much, you cannot touch,
Your child's heart that way,
Oh! it may buy him food or toys,
But you must give him time,
Your time, if you would ever say,
'I've made my child's heart glad.'

Mother, who daily makes the mould
In those first years, edged by fears,
Fears of how he'll fare,
Make yours the encouraging word,
And hold his love, even when he rebels,
Always care, always care,
And you'll make your child's heart glad.

Then when he's left his parents' care,
Leaving the nest, and the rest,
To make his own,
When you are old and that childhood's gone,
Far from your grasp and reach,
He'll say of you in truth,
'They made my childhood glad'.

If the Lord Jesus gave time to children how could we do less? In the time we spend with them let it not always be play but let us take time to teach them the Scriptures, to speak of the Lord Jesus and, of course, to pray with them. I warrant a mother and father that prayers are of more value than gold.

But childhood passes and with it childish things. The young believer must be encouraged to grow up, to go on to spiritual manhood or womanhood and to fulfil all the potential which God has for them. A patent biblical example of this is Peter. No one had played a more vital role in the spiritual history of the world. He is mentioned in the New Testament one hundred and sixty times and his character is one of the most vividly and charmingly drawn in all of the Bible. This eager, impulsive, self-confident, aggressive and daring man was also unstable, fickle, weak and cowardly. Pre-eminently a man of action, liable to inconsistency and rashness, Peter was moulded by the Lord Jesus into one of the greatest Christians of all time. Peter became a pillar of the church,[2] wrote two epistles of great encouragement for those enduring persecution and will for always be remembered as the most lovable and prominent of the twelve apostles. The interesting thing to note is how clearly and deliberately the Lord Jesus spent time with Peter. By the sea of Galilee as he was casting nets with his brother Andrew, a simple word holds a real key to the meaning behind all the time Jesus took with Peter. *'Come after me'*, said the Lord Jesus, *'and I will make you become fishers of men.'*[3] Peter, the mighty fisher of men on the day of Pentecost, with thousands of fish in his nets, is not made overnight. *'I will make you become'*, is the key. Encouragement and training take time.

Spending Time with Peter

For three years Peter is given, again and again, time with the Lord in his inner circle. The Lord was singling him out for a very special reason. At the house of Jairus Peter is given a rare privilege to watch the Saviour raise a teenage girl from the dead? Compare the two passages and meditate on them. Meditate particularly on the similarities.

'And he permitted no one to follow him except Peter, James, and John the brother of James. Then he came to the house of

the ruler of the synagogue, and saw a tumult and those who wept and wailed loudly. When he came in, he said to them, "Why make this commotion and weep? The child is not dead, but sleeping".

And they laughed him to scorn. But when he had put them all out, he took the father and the mother of the child, and those who were with him, and entered where the child was lying. Then he took the child by the hand, and said to her, "Talitha, Cumi!" which is translated, "little girl, I say to you, arise". Immediately the girl arose and walked, for she was twelve years of age. And they were overcome with great amazement.'⁴

'At Joppa there was a certain disciple named Tabitha, which is translated Dorcas. This woman was full of good works and charitable deeds which she did. But it happened in those days that she became sick and died. When they had washed her, they laid her in an upper room. And since Lydda was near Joppa, and the disciples had heard that Peter was there, they sent two men to him, imploring him not to delay in coming to them.

Then Peter arose and went with them. When he had come, they brought him to the upper room. And all the widows stood by him weeping, showing the tunics and garments which Dorcas had made while she was with them.

But Peter put them all out, and knelt down and prayed. And turning to the body he said, "Tabitha, arise." And she opened her eyes, and when she saw Peter she sat up. Then he gave her his hand and lifted her up; and when he had called the saints and widows, he presented her alive.

And it became known throughout all Joppa, and many believed on the Lord.'⁵

Encouragement Is Perpetuated

The point is that in a ministry of encouragement time taken to teach and encourage young believers leaves its mark on their lives. It did on Peter's. Your encouragement will be perpetuated. If, as the book of Proverbs states, we *'train up a child in the way he should go, even when he is old he will not depart from it'*, [6] then the perpetuity of encouragement of believers carries the very same principle.

A lad stood on the railway station, weeping. He had lost his ticket. A man standing close at hand and seeing the situation came over and kindly bought him one. 'When you are grown up', he counselled the boy, 'You will one day come across a boy in similar circumstances as yourself. Will you promise that you will do for him as I have done for you?' As the train pulled out of the station the lad shouted out of the open carriage window 'I'll pass it on sir. I'll pass it on.' That act is probably still circulating the world somewhere this very day.

Peter was singled out from within an inner circle to witness the transformation of the Lord Jesus. His well-intentioned blunder of putting Moses and Elijah on a similar level to the Lord was quickly set right when the voice said to him *'This is my beloved Son, hear him!'* What an encouragement that special time of viewing the glory of the Lord was for Peter! There was no greater exponent of the deity of Christ in history than the big fisherman. It was Peter who said, *'You are the Christ, the Son of the living God.'* [7] Listen to him in the first great recorded Gospel message of the church age: the city is Jerusalem, the time is the feast of Pentecost:

'Therefore let all the house of Israel know assuredly that God has made this Jesus, whom you crucified, both Lord and Christ.' [8]

Read his words written to persecuted Christians:

> 'For we did not follow cunningly devised fables when we made known to you the power and coming of our Lord Jesus Christ, but were eye-witnesses of his majesty.
>
> For he received from God the Father honour and glory when such a voice came to him from the Excellent Glory: "This is my beloved Son, in whom I am well pleased."
>
> And we heard this voice which came from heaven when we were with him on the holy mountain.'9

That special time spent with Christ on the mountain influenced millions through Peter and made him the great defender of Christ's deity.

After Peter's awful denial of his Lord in the house of the high priest and his defection back to the fishing trade it is most touching to read how the Saviour encouraged Peter back to his service. He did not call Peter to a series of meetings on back-sliding or a seminar on the new covenant! Jesus met with Peter on the shores of Tiberias, overflowed his nets with the fish Peter's vain efforts could not catch and then he cooked him some. Christ fed him and then led him to repentance. Then the Lord added a most significant word.

> ' "When you were younger, you girded yourself and walked where you wished; but when you are old, you will stretch out your hands, and another will gird you and carry you where you do not wish." This he spoke, signifying by what death he would glorify God.'10

The time spent encouraging Peter at the sea of Tiberias greatly bolstered him for the grim prophecy of his martyrdom. Many years pass and now he knows, as he writes his last letter, that his death is approaching, and he in turn encourages his fellow believers.

> 'Yes I think it is right, as long as I am in this tent (life), to stir you up by reminding you, knowing that shortly I must "die", just as our Lord Jesus Christ showed me.'[11]

As with Peter, so it will be in all our lives. Those people we spend time with, encouraging them, will be deeply influenced by it to the end of their days. Think of Rachel's influence on Joseph, of Elizabeth on John the Baptist, of Monica on Augustine, of Suzannah on John Wesley, of EJH Nash on an almost seventeen year-old John Stott, of George McDonald on CS Lewis. The list is endless. Who encouraged you? I gladly bear witness to the influence of my dear mother who read the Word to me, prayed with me, counselled and encouraged me to live for the Lord Jesus.

Can we estimate the role of mothers in terms of influence? If they are real encouragers then the extent of their influence in incalculable. Evangelise a woman and you evangelise a family, and families make up the world's population!

The angel did not say 'Go and tell his disciples – and Peter'[12] for nothing. Who is *your* Peter?

But what of the Lord's first call to Peter? '*I will make you become fishers of men*' was the promise: to him all those years with the Lord were an encouragement towards the goal of evangelism. Did he become a fisherman of souls? Can we learn anything from Peter about how we can in turn encourage others to trust in our Lord Jesus?

The Complete Angler

It was Isaak Walton the great English angler who said that

the complete angler must first keep himself well out of sight when fishing. The hidden angler is a successful fisherman. There was a lot of Peter in sight when he left Galilee to fish for men. *'Even if all are made to stumble, yet I will not be'*, he boasted to the Lord. But he learned to hide himself when fishing for Jesus and one has only to read his letters and trace his influence in the New Testament to see that he became a humble man.

There are a lot of people who are frightened away from the Gospel because those who proclaim it are too much to the fore. Christian evangelistic services are often the very place where non christians are frightened away downstream by the angler on the platform! Instead of using the bait of God's word he talks about himself to the hiding of the Saviour. This does not mean that anecdotes of personal experience in personal or public witness are not effective: they are very effective. Paul began his greatest Gospel book, the letter to the Romans, with the words *'I, Paul'*. It is when the man hides his bait with too much of himself that fish flip their tails and go away in shoals.

Isaak Walton wrote that secondly, an angler must keep his face to the sun and then his shadow will not frighten the fish. An angler could be hidden but he could cast a long shadow. I'm afraid Peter's shadow frightened many a soul. As the fire crackled on the night of the Saviour's awful treatment at the hands of the high priest Peter's curses filled the air. Never was a shadow darker. When the Light of the World turned in his direction and looked at him and Peter's face was turned toward that light, how different! He went out and wept bitterly and repented thoroughly. How many a person has been frightened away from spiritual things because of the dark shadows cast by Christians? Let's keep our faces toward the light!

Of course, Walton warned, a good angler must study the

curious ways of fish. He must know where they love to congregate. He must know what their interests are. He must realise their dislikes. He must know his fish if he wants to catch them.

Christian fishermen sometimes go fishing for souls without the slightest clue that different fish have different personalities and ways.

Was Jesus' approach to Nicodemus the same as his 'casting' with the woman at the well? Was his angling for Paul the same as that for Peter? He knew the men and women he sought to bring to himself. His bait, though the same, was 'cast in different ways'. And anglers must be patient. Very patient. They might not catch that fish today but they may tomorrow afternoon. It may rain today and tomorrow afternoon may be all sunshine but the angler must be patient.

The Lord Jesus took a lot of time with Peter to encourage him. But it was worth it. Let us all learn to fish for souls in the world's great waters in our own generation. And, if you would fish like Peter:

> *'Keep yourself well out of sight.*
> *Know the fishes' curious ways.*
> *Keep your face toward the light.*
> *And study patience all your days.'*

Notes

1. Genesis 21.8
2. Galatians 2.9
3. Mark 1.27
4. Mark 5.37–42
5. Acts 9.36–42
6. Proverbs 22.6
7. Matthew 16.16

8. Acts 2.36
9. 2 Peter 1.16–18
10. John 21.18–19
11. 2 Peter 1.13–14
12. Mark 16.7

10: Hinges

When Dr Barbara McClintock won the 1983 Nobel Prize for Medicine she did not receive a morning call from Stockholm, she does not have a phone. She heard the news on the radio and is said to have mumbled 'Oh dear', donned her baggy dungarees and stepped out for her usual morning walk through the woods near Cold Spring Harbour Laboratory on Long Island. The eighty-one year-old geneticist is quite a lady. She now takes her place with just six other women in the eighty-two years of Nobel history, including Marie Curie for discovering radium, and Dorothy Crowfoot for deciphering the structure of penicillin.

I was fascinated to discover that Barbara McClintock's life was hardly one of encouragement along the way. The third of four children born to a Hartford doctor and his wife, she enrolled when she was seventeen at Cornell University, despite her mother's conviction that college was no place for a woman. She intended to major in plant-breeding but had to opt for botany because plant-breeding was considered unsuitable for ladies. She earned her doctorate in plant genetics but because tenured faculty positions were not available to women in the 1930s she bounced from job to job.

It was the Carnegie Institution of Washington DC which came to her rescue and gave her a job at its genetics laboratory in Cold Spring Harbour. She has been there ever since, grateful for their encouragement. *'If I had been at some other place, I'm sure that I would've been fired for what I was doing,'* she noted recently, *'because nobody was accepting it.'*

The Carnegie Institute Genetic Department was the hinge on which the great scientist swung! They stayed with her even when she soon fell from the graces of her peers. The idea that genes could 'jump' around on a chromosome flew in the face of scientific dogma. *'They thought I was crazy, absolutely mad,'* she recalls. Not so now. Dr McClintock is recognised as making one of the greatest discoveries of our times in genetics, affecting medical knowledge of how bacteria develop resistance to an antibiotic, amongst many other things. No one thinks of genetics now without the implications of her work. They are glad they encouraged Barbara down at Cold Spring Harbour. The laboratory there was a little hinge for a very big and useful door!

When the late Sir Ralph Richardson went for his first audition speech, the repertory company manager said, 'It's frightful, Richardson; you could never, never be any good as Falstaff.' The next time Ralph Richardson slipped into that role he was proclaimed the greatest Falstaff in living memory! I'm sure that company manager is sorry he had not been a better hinge.

Little hinges! It is the little things in life which make life swing. Think about them. A smile. A note of appreciation. A song. A chat with someone with a similar problem to mine. A mature person admitting that they actually do have problems! A friendly handshake. A small gift. A friend calling in. Another driver letting me out of a tight situation and being courteous about it. Rainbows. A baby's hand. The list is fascinating.

Let's examine three hinges upon which a great ministry of encouragement can swing.

The Hinge of Meals!

Elijah the great prophet is depressed. He feels so bad that he wants to die. Tired and deeply discouraged in God's work he sits down under a juniper tree and moans that he is no better than his forefathers. How does God encourage his discouraged servant? He sends an angel to give him a meal, twice. Have you ever thought of the ministry of a meal as a source of encouragement?

Food gives us strength. It makes us feel healthy and at ease. It also is a time for talking to people, for getting closer. Have you ever noticed how folk linger around a table after a meal, talking? There are lots of ways for using meals as a blessing to others. Why not use that bedsitter tray, that kitchen corner, that hotel suite to give a meal as a source of fellowship and encouragement to someone in need of it today? That new mother next door who had her first baby last week does not really feel like cooking a lot this week; why not take a few meals around to her? I have been given free meal vouchers by a friend to give meals to people who need encouragement and many a heart-breaking problem has been solved over such meals. Surroundings, however, are not really all that important. I have been given a meal from a hole in the ground in Asia before now: how very refreshing and encouraging the food was that afternoon! Earlier in his career God fed Elijah by the brook Cherith, and sent him a waiter in black tails.[1] Later an angel fed him by a tree. Either way, the prophet was encouraged.

Study meal times in the Bible and you'll find that they played a vital part in history. The Lord Jesus ate and drank with people in order to witness to them. Daniel by his meal times witnessed to a nation, particularly by what he ate. Didn't Abraham and Sarah give a meal to three strangers and discover that they were angels from heaven? Be careful how you treat that stranger at your table next week: he might be an angel.[2] Wasn't love captured at a meal in Bethlehem between the beautiful Ruth and the wealthy Boaz?[3] How did David fulfil his promise to his dearest friend Jonathan who had been slain in battle? He ensured that Jonathan's son ate at his table continually.[4]

Surely there is a very potent symbol of fellowship behind the Lord using 'the breaking of bread' to institute 'The Lord's Supper' and 'the drinking of the cup' as a remembrance of his death. Meals are a very vital part of our lives and they can be used as sources of great encouragement in the Lord's hands. Remember what God did with the little lad's five barley loaves and two small fish. What could he not do with our coffee, tea, steaks, tomatoes, peas and trifles if they were given into his hands!

But you may not be a restaurant owner or a bedsitter occupant. You may not own a house let alone have a kitchen of your own. Perhaps no door of encouragement could swing on the hinge of your cooking or meals. Truth is you may not be able to cook or to be Shirley Conran's 'Superwoman', but are you useful with a pen or an encouraging turn of phrase? How about lifting the phone and ringing someone in need to tell them you were thinking about them? I have a friend who rings me up on the telephone and prays with me. Maybe one of these days when we get a crossed line the amazed 'listener-in' will get converted! Use the telephone to show your appreciation for something someone has done or to pass on some encouragement from God's Word to a friend in need of it. We honestly have not yet calculated the immense influence of what we say to each other.

The Hinge of Letters

For me one of the saddest things happening is the fact that letter writing is fast becoming a lost art. Professor Marshall McLuhan stated that television was going to outlive writing, but the amazing thing is that he had to write a book to try to convince everybody![5] When God wanted to communicate with us, in every generation, he wrote to us.

There once lived a man who had very bad eyesight and who had no way of getting reading glasses. *'See with what large letters I have written to you with my own hand.'* he wrote to the Galatians.[6] (Meaning 'See what large letters I used as I wrote to you with my own hand.') The man who once carried letters of the high priest to the synagogues of Damascus in order to put them in prison turned out to be the greatest letter-writer the christian world has ever known. He wrote letters to Christians to fire and encourage them on for God in language never to be surpassed. Millions of people still read them every day. They were God-breathed letters.

Letters of sheer encouragement have tremendous effect. The media crave for them and when Christians write as they should to the media to discourage radio and television producers from the poor material they frequently offer, we should encourage them to produce something better. When they *do* so, let us *say* so. The word *'congratulations'* is not hard to write. Can you imagine what five hundred thousand letters would do to a producer if they landed on his desk tomorrow? Christians may appear to be cross-eyed discus throwers and cross-eyed discus throwers may not score many points, but, *'they sure keep the crowd awake!'*

Why not keep your eye on the newspaper and watch for someone who has done something worthwhile? Write to him or her. Say '*Well done!*' You would be surprised how few do it.

> '*In life's dying embers, I have two regrets,*
> *When I'm right, no one remembers,*
> *When I'm wrong, no one forgets*'

A little letter, what a small hinge it may seem; upon it a great matter may depend. Take the work of Florence Nightingale. When I see the dedication of the nursing profession I think of Dr Ward Hewe's letter to Florence who had spoken of her 'unusual' desire to 'nurse' wounded men in Crimea.

> '*My dear Miss Florence,*
>   *It would be unusual and in England whatever is unusual is thought to be unsuitable; but I say to you . . . if you have a vocation for that way of life, act up to your inspiration and you will find there is never anything unbecoming in doing your duty for the good of others. Choose, go on with it, wherever it may lead you and God be with you.*' – And he was and the whole world knows the result.

But, you may quickly add, 'I'm no cook but the problem is I'm no writer either!' Perhaps you say that it would take you a week to get a letter written. How, then, about the ability to say 'Thank you?' 'I'm shy,' you add. That's no disqualification – look what shyness has done for the Princess of Wales! There are lots of ways to say thank you. The Lord Jesus was deeply touched by the one out of the ten lepers who took the time to come back and say 'thank you'. If the Creator is moved by the creature returning thanks, wouldn't your word of thanks be appreciated by the canteen lady, the taxi driver, the shop assistant, the receptionist, or a dozen other people who serve you daily?

A New Way to Say 'Thank You'

One very special way of witnessing through saying 'Thank you' has been put out by the Christian Publicity Organisation in the form of most attractive little 'Thank you' cards. This tiny card has a pastoral scene on one side with the words 'Thank you' printed on it. On the other side is a space where you can have your name and telephone number inserted below these printed words:

'Thank you for your helpful and efficient service. It was much appreciated'.
Did you know that in serving others you follow the best possible example? The Bible says that Jesus 'took the nature of a servant' when he came to earth. He told his friends that he had 'not come to be served but to serve and to give up his life as a ransom for many.' Jesus left the glory of heaven to serve humanity. He loved you so much that he gave his life to put you right with God. Today he wants to come into your life and give it direction and purpose. He wants you to become the person you were always meant to be. Would you like to know more? I'd be glad to help you'.[7]

These cards can be an excellent way to leave a word of witness behind you. I have seen people react in amazing ways to them. One day I was standing by a lift in a large store in a large city. There was no way of knowing whether the lift was functioning or not so I asked a lady standing by if it was working.

'Oh yes!' she answered immediately. I waited and it was.

We all piled in and when we arrived at the correct floor I passed the elevator operator a 'thank you' card. Suddenly I heard a most irritated voice behind me say to her husband, 'Did you see *that*? He gave the elevator lady one but the person who told him it was working doesn't get one!' There followed a rather sarcastic laugh. What did I do? I quickly shoved my hand in my pocket, located a 'thank you' card, gave her one and virtually ran for my life! Oh the power of the word 'thank you.'

Recently I felt greatly humbled before God. A young lady came to talk after a service and pointed out that I had left a little 'thank you' card on her cashiers desk after purchasing a kitchen clock from her section of a large department store. I had forgotten all about it. She hadn't. It had led to her conversion! I seldom look at that clock on our kitchen wall, but I thank God for those little 'thank you' cards.

Saying 'thank you' can mean so much. At Christmas the people of Norway say thank you to the people of Britain for their help in the Second World War by sending a tall Christmas tree to Trafalgar Square. It is only a Christmas tree, but there is a nation's spirit behind its presence. Even a small flower arrangement sent to a hospital ward can say so much. *Some people would send a lorry-load of flowers to your funeral but they wouldn't send one daffodil to you while you are alive.* (I'd better watch what I'm writing because recently I said this in public and a family arrived at my door with one carefully wrapped daffodil!)

So, if you feel you want to write or say thank you in some way, do it now. *Don't wait till he's dead.*

The Hinge of Feeling Wanted

Recently a friend of mine was rung up on the phone in the middle of the night. A husband was desperately wanting help for his wife who was ill and who needed help, fast.

When my friend arrived at the home the patient protested profusely for having bothered her at such an hour. *'Don't rob me of the joy of feeling wanted,'* was the reply.

The hinge of feeling needed and wanted is a very important hinge to the door of life. When people become isolated from others they are in trouble. Depression, paranoia, schizophrenia, rape, suicide and a wide variety of states of disease show that isolation is the destructive influence on physical and mental health.

There is a book called *The One Minute Manager* which advocates that all managers take at least one minute every day with each of their employees to encourage them in some aspect of the work they have done or are doing. Just one minute per day. What a surprise it would cause on many a 'shop' floor if that happened every day. It would make employees feel wanted and appreciated in an increasingly automatised environment.

In the life of Paul the apostle there is an incident which shows this important hinge in life swinging into action. Can there ever have been a more welcome crowd than the Christians who walked forty-three miles out of Rome on the Appian Way, the great road from Rome to the Bay of Naples, just to meet and encourage Paul as he came under Roman guard to plead his case to Caesar? Those Christians didn't need to go and they certainly were not expected, but few could have been more encouraged than Paul at their presence. He had just been shipwrecked off Malta and had previously known great persecution for his faith. Those people who waited for Paul at the Appi Forum on the Appian Way did not wait until Paul was dead to honour him. They encouraged him just when he needed them most. *'When Paul saw them'*, records Dr Luke, *'he thanked God and took courage'*.[8]

'Encourage him!' said Moses to the people of Israel (Make him feel wanted!) *'Encourage him and strengthen him, for he shall go over before his people and he shall cause them to inherit the land which you will see.'*[9] Whether it be Joshua or Paul, Christians in Katmandu or believers in Pucket's Creek, we all need encouragement. So let's oil the hinges. Let's start doing one or two things daily to encourage others. Whether it is a meal, a phone call, a letter, a card, a one-minute word of appreciation, a facility loaned, whatever, let's do it *today*. If someone is tolerant, praise them for it, if someone is thorough, commend them, if tactfulness has been shown, comment.

I listened recently to one of the 'all time greats' in the golfing world, Bobby Locke. He was speaking of another 'all time great' whom he reckoned had one searing fault. 'Why, he would go around the course in a competition,' said Mr Locke, 'and when his opponent did well he would never say a word. My dear old Dad used to always teach me that when playing competitive golf and your partner plays a good shot, say 'good shot!'

Such an act is one of the most important hinges to a life of usefulness, and it does not just apply to a golf course, does it?

Notes

1. 1 Kings 17.4
2. Hebrews 13.2
3. Ruth 2.14
4. 2 Samuel 9.7
5. Professor Marshall McLuhan, Founder of the Centre for Culture and Technology at the University of Toronto, died 1980.
6. Galatians 6.11

7. Christian Publicity Organisation, Ivy Arch Rd, Worthing, England. Write for free sample of their excellent material.
8. Acts 28.15
9. Deuteronomy 1.37–38
10. Deuteronomy 3.28

11: Going the Second Mile

John Wesley once wrote to a young preacher to encourage him. In his letter Wesley gave the preacher an encouraging verse of Scripture but at the same time slipped a few notes of money into the envelope.

The young preacher on receiving Wesley's letter replied, pointing out that he always enjoyed the verses of Scripture Mr Wesley gave but never had he quite so enjoyed expository notes! Mr Wesley was what I would call a second miler.

On arriving in New York for the first time, I had a ride in a famed New York taxi cab and said, naively, to the New York 'cabbie' as I was paying him, '*That was my first ride in a New York taxi cab.*' We usually expect a forty cent tip, sir', he said. He was definitely not a second miler!

I am, of course, using the phrase 'a second miler' as indicating a generous spirit which in every circumstance goes beyond the call of duty to help and encourage. In the context of the Sermon on the Mount it has an explicit application. The Lord Jesus said, '*and whoever compels you to go one mile, go with him two.*'[1] Israel was occupied by the Romans and soldiers were constantly moving all over the place. When a Roman soldier was moving across the country he would take some able-bodied man and compel him to carry his military baggage for him:

'To protect those who lived in occupied territory from the Roman soldiers' right to requisition burden bearers the Roman law said the soldier could conscript a civilian to carry his burden for only one mile. Then the man was to be released and the soldier would have to find someone else or carry the burden himself. Our Lord said that if someone conscripted you to carry his burden the required mile and you came to the end of the mile and the soldier released you, you should gladly carry it further. The conscripted one had his rights. They were protected by law but he had the right to give up his rights to manifest the righteousness of Christ.'[2]

Having covered a lot of ground on the subject of encouragement in this book, it is time for us to really catch the *spirit* of the subject, to epitomise it. For me the second miler is the one who characterises all I have been trying to say. Rare he or she might be, but what a track record they have! We want now to draw inspiration from those who give that little bit extra that makes all the difference: a marathon of second milers if you like!

Eric Liddell Was a Second Miler

History is full of stories of people who at great personal sacrifice have gone beyond the call of duty. Captain L E G Oates heroically walked out into a blizzard on Scott's last great expedition to the South Pole in March 1912. Oates' condition had been hindering the progress of the expedition party and he hoped that his sacrifice would allow the others to push on faster. There was the great politician Ghandi and his immense commitment to independence for India and the sacrifice he gave in hunger and humiliation to see his dreams fulfilled. There was Eric Liddell who, as a brilliant athlete, refused to run in an Olympic final because it was being held on the Lord's day but who played football with young people in a Japanese prisoner-of-war camp on the Lord's day, to prevent them from falling into all kinds of evil with so much spare time on their hands. The latter action tells as much about the wonderful man as the former. It is fascinating that such selfless acts have become the basis for film makers in the last few years and have been sweeping Hollywood Oscars before them. There were not many Oscars given out at the time the acts were committed!

Modern life has shown 'second milers' too. Every now and again a selfless act of someone going the second mile in their duty crosses international barriers and draws admiration from everyone. There was Colonel H. Jones who put into practice what he expected others to do and gave his life in the Falklands conflict in 1982. Shall we ever forget the man who plunged into the frozen Potomac River in Washington to save the lady who was drowning after an Air Florida jet had crashed into the river? Others were standing around doing their duty on the edge of the river operating the rescue but he plunged in from the edge. He had every right to stay where he was but he waived his rights in order to save a drowning woman.

In his tremendous book, *Quality Friendship*, Gary Inrig wrote:

> '*In 1928 a very interesting case came before the courts in the state of Massachusetts. It concerned a man who had been walking on a boat dock when suddenly he tripped over a rope and fell into the cold, deep water of an ocean bay. He came up spluttering and yelling for help and then sank again, obviously in trouble. His friends were too far away to get to him but only a few yards away, on another dock,*

*was a young man sprawled on a deckchair, sunbathing.
"Help! I can't swim!" came the desperate shout. The young
man, an excellent swimmer, only turned his head to watch
as the man floundered in the water, sank, came up
spluttering in total panic and then disappeared forever.*

*The family of the drowned man were so upset by that
display of callous indifference that they sued the sunbather.
They* LOST. *The court reluctantly ruled that the man on the
dock had no legal responsibility whatever to try and save the
other man's life.'*[3]

Learn from the Devil

God's law is different. *'Do not withold good from those to
whom it is due, when it is in the power of your hand to do so.
Do not say to your neighbour, "Go, and come back, and
tomorrow I will give it", when you have it with you.'*[4] We
must not wait to go the second mile. Why? Because another
second miler is very busy. Who is he? Let Hugh Latimer
explain in the words of his most famous sermon preached in
St Paul's Cathedral on January 18, 1548, soon after he had
been released from the Tower of London:

'And now I would ask you a strange question; who is the
most diligent bishop and prelate in all England; that passes
all the rest in doing his office? I can tell you for I know who
it is: I know him well. But now I think I see you listening
and hearkening that I should name him. He is the most
diligent prelate and preacher in all England. And will ye
know who it is? I will tell you – it is the Devil. He is the
most diligent preacher of all others: he is never out of his
diocese; he is never from his cure; you shall never find him
unoccupied: he is ever in his parish; he keeps residence at
all times: you shall never find him idle, I warrant you . . .
Where the devil is resident and has his plough going, there,

away with books and up with candles; away with Bibles and
up with beads; away with the light of the Gospel and up
with the light of candles, yea, at noonday; . . . up with
man's traditions and his laws, down with God's traditions
and his most holy Word; . . . oh that our prelates would be
as diligent . . . the prelates . . . are lords and no labourers;
but the devil is diligent at his plough. He is no unpreaching
prelate; he is no lordly loiterer from his cure; but a busy
ploughman . . . Therefore, ye unpreaching prelates, learn
of the devil: to be diligent in doing of your office . . . If you
will not learn of God, nor good men, to be diligent in your
office, learn of the devil.'[5]

The immediate commitment to go the second mile for
God is the great mark of truly spiritual people. They are
well aware that Satan is busy so they get busy too. There is
urgency in it. There is no holding back. David Lloyd
George once said that a certain British Member of
Parliament had *'sat so long on the fence the iron had entered
into his soul.'* Truly spiritual people have no such iron in
their souls. They do not reduce the great commission of the
Lord Jesus to *'Go into all the world and make disciples of all
nations and if you don't manage it, I died for them anyway, so
it will be all right somehow'*, wrote Dick Dowsett. *'So then'*,
he adds, *'it's not surprising that with hell forgotten, the social,
economic and political needs of the nations are given more
immediate importance than their need to hear the Gospel and
be converted.'*[6]

Chasing Giants at Eighty-Five!

Let me pick out a few of the galaxy of people in the
Scriptures who went the second mile for God. Think of
Miriam, Moses' sister. Sent to watch her baby brother as he
lay in the ark of bullrushes she saw Pharaoh's daughter

compassionately lift the crying child. She could have stayed in hiding, kept quiet and not risked her life but she went beyond the call of duty and told Pharaoh's daughter where she could find a nurse for the baby and brought him home! Thus did Miriam ensure a godly upbringing for what proved to be one of the very greatest leaders the world has ever known.

Caleb's courage is legendary. When he and his friend Joshua were faced with moaners by the thousand who demurred from advancing into Canaan on hearing that giants and walled cities lay in their path, these two men of God cried, '*Let us go up at once and take possession for we are well able to overcome!*'[7] Their encouragement fell on deaf ears. Because Israel adopted the majority report God imposed upon them forty years 'wandering' in the wilderness till that generation should die out. What is so challenging about Caleb is that forty five years later at the age of eighty five, and now in Canaan for his faithfulness, he asked for Hebron at the distribution of land. Hebron?! Hebron and the hill country were the places where the fearful Anakim lived who had terrorised ten of the spies. He courageously took possession of it and drove out the three sons of Anak in 1444 BC. It is obvious that Caleb was a second miler of tremendous agility and faith and still going as strong as ever at eighty-five. There is no retirement in God's work.

Beauty and Brains

And Abigail, what of her? When David rounded up his men and set off to murder Abigail's husband Nabal for his despicable treatment of David's cause she did not say, 'I told you so'. There was none of the '*Well now, this young man with all his poetry and preaching and psalm singing is just*

*like the rest of them. What can I do about it? I can't stop him
and remind him that a wrong doesn't make a right despite my
wicked husband's behaviour.'* No; Abigail went the second
mile for the Lord in encouraging a wayward David back on
to God's way for him.

> *'Then Abigail made haste and took two hundred loaves of
> bread, two skins of wine, five sheep ready dressed, five seahs
> of roasted grain, one hundred clusters of raisins and two
> hundred cakes of figs, and loaded them on donkeys . . . and
> fell on her face before David and said: "On me, my lord, on
> me let this iniquity be! . . . Please, let not my lord regard
> this scoundrel Nabal . . . and now this present which your
> maidservant has brought to my lord, let it be given to the
> young men who follow my lord . . . for the Lord will
> certainly make for my lord an enduring house . . . and the
> lives of your enemies he shall sling out, as from the pocket of
> a sling. And it shall come to pass, when the Lord has done
> for my lord according to all the good that he has spoken
> concerning you and has appointed you ruler over Israel, that
> this will be no grief to you, nor offense of heart to my lord,
> either that you have shed blood without cause, or that my
> lord has avenged himself." '*[8]

She had beauty and brains, did Abigail, and she put them to
good use. Going the second mile can empty your kitchen
cupboards but God will see to it that they will be filled to
overflowing; soon Abigail was in charge of the palace
kitchens! (Compare Michal's behaviour in 2 Samuel
6.16–23).

It seems that Solomon, under God, had inherited his
father's literary gift, and being wise he did not let it lie
dormant but went the second mile with his pen. He wrote
three thousand proverbs and one thousand and five songs

including the incredibly beautiful Song of Songs and two Psalms (Psalms 72 and 127). Solomon's pathetic uselessness at the end of his life warns us that second-milers for God can become second-milers for the devil in a very short space of time. None of us are exempt.

I was sitting around a friend's fireside the other night and we were overhauling the universe together. My friend's boy, Richard, was present and drawing him into the conversation I asked, 'Richard, who do you think was a second-miler in the Bible?' Like a flash the ten-year-old lad said, 'The woman who gave all she had.' He was right. The Saviour had been watching at the seat of the Treasury and said that the woman gave more than all the rest because she gave all that she had. She was a second-miler in giving. Have any of us ever lost by giving to God? Give Him a teaspoonful and he will give you back shovelfuls. As Jim Elliot of Ecuador said, '*He is no fool who gives what he cannot keep to gain what he cannot lose.*'

The New Testament is filled with second-milers. What about the fellows who got the man to the Saviour through a hole in the roof? What about the lad who gave his lunch to the Master and saw thousands fed? What about Joseph of Arimathaea who gave his tomb to a crucified Lord Jesus and found his grave the most famous one in the history of the world because the Saviour rose again from it? What of Lydia whose heart the Lord opened? We have already mentioned how she opened her house to Paul and Silas, and Philippi was opened to the Gospel and then Europe was opened to the good news! A second-miler became God's highway to a continent.

There are few who have gone the second mile for God like Paul did. Let him tell us about it:

'*In labours more abundant, in stripes above measure, in*

prisons more frequently, in deaths often. From the Jews five times I received forty stripes minus one. Three times I was beaten with rods; once I was stoned; three times I was shipwrecked; a night and a day I have been in the deep; in journeys often, in perils of waters, in perils of robbers, in perils of my own countrymen, in perils of the Gentiles, in perils in the city, in perils in the wilderness, in perils in the sea, in perils among false brethren: in weariness and toil, in sleeplessness often, in hunger and thirst, in fastings often, in cold and nakedness, besides the other things, what comes upon me daily: my deep concern for all the churches . . . The God and Father of our Lord Jesus Christ, who is blessed for ever, knows I am not lying.'[9]

Parsley on Top

So here's to the second milers. Here's to men who hand out hymn books at church services with a handshake and a welcoming smile thrown in; to Sunday-school teachers who not only teach John 3. 16 to their classes but have the children up 'to tea and toast and cake' now and again. Here's to hosts who say to the visiting preacher after he comes in exhausted, 'Would you like to have supper in bed, brother, and the electric blanket is on! There's a stack of *National Geographics* and a few copies of *Homes and Gardens* up there too!' Here's to preachers who shake your hand before going in to their service rather than on the way out. Here's to the host of men and women who go to no end of trouble to ensure that all hear the Gospel of Jesus Christ and to wives who change the furniture around now and again and put some fresh green parsley on top of the soup. Here's to airline pilots who tell you a little more than what the weather is like in the city you are flying to or what is coming up on the other side of the jet from the side you are sitting on and to churches who are determined that there is more to the Gospel than 'seven to eight' on a Sunday evening in the form of a hymn, a prayer, a hymn, announcements, a sermon, a prayer, a hymn and so to bed. Here especially is to those who when they are squeezed by life's pressures are like Fred Lemon, the ex-burglar, now a christian author, preacher and greengrocer; 'What do you get when you squeeze an orange, Derick?', he asked me one day.

'You get orange juice', I replied.

'What do you get when you squeeze a lemon?', he questioned again.

'You get lemon juice', I replied.

'No', said Fred Lemon in his famous Cockney accent, 'when you squeeze a lemon you get Jesus!'

Here's to all who when they see a genuine need are ready to give all possible genuine help. Here's to all who encourage people before they die! '*If we see*', said James, '*a brother or sister is naked and destitute of daily food and one of you says to them, "Depart in peace, be warmed and filled", but you do not give them the things which are needed for the body, what does it profit?*'[10] It obviously profits nothing. How can we hold '*the faith of our Lord Jesus Christ, the Lord of glory*'[11] and not be a second-miler? After all did he not (and most reverently I write it) go the second mile for us? We started this book with the thought of being conformed to his image. Let's end with it.

I gave him a crown of thorns,

He gave me a crown of righteousness.

I gave him a cross to carry,

He gave me his yoke which is easy, his burden which is light.

I gave him nails through his hands,

He gave me safely into his father's hands from which no power can pluck me.

I gave him a mock title, 'This is the King of the Jews'.

He gave me a new name and made me a king and a priest to God.

I gave him no covering, stripping his clothes from him,

He gave me a garment of salvation.

I gave him mockery, casting the same in his teeth,

He gave me Paradise.

I gave him vinegar to drink,

He gave me Living Water.

I crucified and slew him on a tree,

He gave me eternal life.

It was my sinfulness that put him there.

It is his sinlessness that puts me here.

Notes

1. Matthew 5.41
2. J Dwight Pentecost: *The Sermon on the Mount: Contemporary Insights For A Christian Lifestyle* (Multnomah Press, 1975, 1980) p. 119.
3. Gary Inrig: *Quality Friendship: The Risks and Rewards* (Moody Press, Chicago) p. 105.
4. Proverbs 3. 27–28
5. Work of Hugh Latimer, Vol. I pp. 59–78
6. Dick Dowsett: *God, That's Not Fair* (OMF Books 1982), Preface p. 10.
7. Numbers 13. 30
8. 1 Samuel 25. 18–31
9. 2 Corinthians 11. 23–31
10. James 2. 15–16
11. James 2. 1

Sure as Sunrise

Derick Bingham

A book of selected texts and thoughts for each day
that challenges and encourages the reader to commit
himself daily to Christ and his world.
Derick Bingham shares his thoughts as he battles
with the constant stress of Ulster life.

Published in **Pickering Paperbacks**.

Step into the Sunshine

Derick Bingham

Covering a wide range of topics for teenagers – from guilt and shyness to parent problems and clothes – Derick Bingham expresses the way teenagers feel, and gives solid help on combating teen problems.

Published in **Pickering Paperbacks**.

A Sword Bathed in Heaven

Norah Bradford

The moving biography of Robert Bradford, one of Ulster's most outstanding MPs, from his young adulthood to his assassination by the IRA in Belfast. The story is told by Robert Bradford's widow Norah.

Published in **Pickering Paperbacks**.